Rethinking

The Law Of Attraction

By

P.R. Young

P.R. Young/Heartworks
P.O. Box 1733
Durango, Colorado 81302

Cover art by Grady H. Pennington
www.ghpart.com

Rethinking the Law of Attraction/ P.R. Young

ISBN-13: 978-1505665031
ISBN-10: 1505665035

Dedicated to

My Silent Partner

Table of Contents

Acknowledgements

Special thanks to the group of beta readers who read the drafts and offered their perspectives and opinions. Absent such a group, a writer has no inkling whether the thing they've spent so much time on is of any value to anyone else, and if it is, whether it's readable. This need for readers might be especially true for spiritual seekers who have danced in the world as academics. I was fortunate to have a collection of readers representing different perspectives ranging from "familiar with" to "never heard of" the Law of Attraction. Spanning six states and three countries, their diverse world dances—as artists, alternative healers, traditional healer, psychologist, preacher, engineer, realtor, and bar owner—further enriched the mix. Being fortunate to have had these excellent readers in my corner, the final product is quite different from the manuscript they read. Many thanks to this wonderful group: Dr. Susan Barnes, Reverend George Harris, Nora Miller, Daphne Moldowin, Dr. Rob Pennington, Trish Simonton, Heather Snow, Ron Taska, M.D., Manoj Vijayan, and Judy Willgoss. Bless you!

Thanks to StarryVision of Fiverr.com for formatting the interior. Thanks to graphic artist Grady Pennington for putting his fabulous "Rose Colored Glasses" art on the cover. Thanks to Steve Jones, without whose generous computer support and patience I couldn't even begin this project. Thanks to their efforts, even a retired teacher living in an attic can share what she's learned.

Special thanks most certainly go to John Simon, editor, who aligned this work with the rules! Any remaining errors are mine for tinkering after the fact.

Finally, and above all, I thank my Silent Partner, without whom this book would never have happened.

Chapter 1

Why *This* Book?
The Story behind the Story

Why on earth would someone waste their time writing yet another book on The Law of Attraction? It certainly was never my intention. I had written the little paper, the master's thesis, and that should have been the end of it. But I couldn't let it go, couldn't stop reading, couldn't stop thinking about it, and I couldn't stop writing about it. Something drove me to do only this for months after I'd submitted that paper. I didn't question it, just assumed that learning more about this current trend was inevitable, considering who I am.

Seeking the truth—whether in the Bible or other spiritual books, in prayers, tossing coins to read I Ching hexagrams, reading Tarot cards, drawing Runes, or sitting still in meditation—has been the principal driving passion through most of my life. That isn't to say that I'm a scholar in any of these things, not by a long stretch. It was never my intention to be a scholar; I have simply been following my heart.

Despite the different methods used, my intent was always the same: to understand the meaning of life, why I'm here, what the rules for "here" might be, and how I most effectively relate to my Creator. (I do believe in a supreme power.) What I've noticed over forty-plus years is that the method doesn't really matter. I am in contact with Source because I intend to be. That within whom I live and move and have my being is always present, just as I am always part of that All That Is. Having kept journals since I was very young, I can report that all my needs have been met even before I realized I had them, and I have been guided each step of the way . . . when I have listened.

For example, one day, not five minutes after I had begun to walk to town with my little tote bag to pick up mail at the post office, I found myself turning around to get the car. I didn't question why, despite the conflicting desire to walk on that beautiful day, because I had learned many years ago to trust those gentle urgings some call intuition. At the post office I discovered why: I had received a large box and several heavy books, too much bulk and weight for my little tote.

My life is simple.I live in the attic apartment of an old house I bought after a divorce more than thirty years ago. I had been a fashion model in college, but since my twenty-second birthday had cheerfully chosen to disregard that pesky need to keep up with the *Joansies*. Collecting material possessions holding no interest for me, why on earth would *I* be interested in the Law of Attraction?

I wasn't. This book began as a paper assigned in a metaphysics course. The choice of topic initially reflected the observation that my advisor had written a paper on the Law of Attraction (LoA), and I had thought it would be fun for her if I were to take a different tack on the same subject.

In the course of reading everything I could find about it, I heard a prominent metaphysics speaker renounce LoA. Though not a follower of that trend, my inner warrior had nevertheless been engaged; I was determined to prove him wrong, or at least to help him see it differently.

The LoA, as a formula for realizing one's desires, was not new to me. It came to my attention in the mid-70s when I read Esther Hicks' *Abraham Speaks*. From my perspective at the time, shaped by studying metaphysics evenings while I taught days at the local college, the LoA was simply a popularized version of "getting more." Not my thing. I was embarked on a search for truth, the sacred secrets of enlightenment, wisdom that was applicable to my daily life.

My introduction to rules for living my life first came from the Bible, especially the Sermon on The Mount and the stories about Jesus healing the sick and performing miracles. However, I apparently missed the how-tos for manifesting, the practical spirituality, that He said was possible for each of us.

Instead, the influence for spiritual growth and matters of conscious creation, manifesting, came from a college student with a lousy attendance record.

I was a teaching assistant at the University of Texas, Austin, in the early 1970s when this student said she'd start coming to my class if I'd accompany her to one of hers. We attended her Tarot class. The teacher related the story of man's spiritual journey represented by colorful images and glyphs associated with each of twenty-two cards he laid out in progression.

Fascinated, longing to learn more, I subscribed to the esoteric studies the Builders of The Adytum (B.O.T.A.) offered via correspondence. Then, snail mail prevailed; there was no Internet or personal computer, it was all very secretive, and there was a special mystery surrounding my secret strudies that kept me floating high even on the toughest days at the college.

But now that we do have Internet, B.O.T.A. has a Web site on which its purpose is stated as follows.

> Builders of the Adytum is a modern Mystery School. Adytum is the Greek word for Inner Shrine or Holy of Holies. Like Jesus, who many believe was trained in Qabalah, members of the order aspire to build the Inner Temple, to construct the Holy of Holies within. People of all faiths are welcome to study the teachings of this Order. B.O.T.A. recognizes Qabalah as the root of Judaism and Christianity. Its ultimate purpose is to hasten the true Brotherhood of mankind and to make manifest the truth that love is the only real power in the universe.[1]

According to the Builders of the Adytum, the function of the Tarot "is to induce the powerful Expanded States of Consciousness in the individual aspirant that will enable him to cope with life efficiently, to understand the spiritual meaning and significance of his experience and environment and its relation to himself as an Eternal Being."[2] The Tarot was meant to be practical? Intended for daily life? *Hallelujah! My prayers were answered!*

Students were required to memorize "The Pattern on the Trestleboard," a set of eleven statements reproduced in Paul Case's book about Tarot. In those statements, I discovered a different relationship with that "something bigger than I am" than the one I had experienced in the church of my youth. I also learned the secrets of co-creation using the mind.

0. All the power that ever was or will be is here now.

1. I am a center of expression for the primal Will-to-Good, which eternally creates and sustains the universe.

2. Through me its unfailing Wisdom takes form in thought and word.

3. Filled with an Understanding of its perfect law, I am guided, moment-by-moment, along the path of liberation.

4. From the exhaustless riches of its Limitless Substance, I draw all things needful, both spiritual and material.

5. I recognize the manifestation of its undeviating justice in all the circumstances of my life.

6. In all things, great and small, I see the Beauty of the divine expression.

7. Living from that Will, supported by its unfailing wisdom and Understanding, mine is the Victorious Life.

8. I look forward with confidence to the perfect realization of the Eternal Splendor of the Limitless Light.

9. In thought and word and deed, I rest my life, from day to day, upon the sure Foundation of Eternal being.

10. The Kingdom of Spirit is embodied in my flesh.[3]

It's not my purpose to elucidate those statements; others have done so amply and eloquently. Of particular relevance to my study, though, is the first, number "0." Zero has special meaning in the occult, signifying the beginning of everything. As Paul Case described it, "An ellipse, representing the Cosmic Egg, whence come all things."[4] Interpreted by Dr. Ann Davies from a Qabalah perspective, the meaning of that first statement, "All the Power that ever was or ever will be is here now," is: "We are part and parcel of the limitless Absolute Consciousness."[5]

Relevant to my perspective on the popular formulas for success associated with the LoA is the meaning of statement number five, "I recognize the manifestation of its undeviating justice in all the circumstances of my life," which Dr. Davies interprets thus: "That which we *do* is the result of our basic patterns of thinking, feeling, and self-identification. If we think and feel insecurity, then we *act* in such ways as to experience this insecurity in our relationships and/or material conditions. We reap that with which we identify ourselves."[6]

If the language seems severe—*manifestation of its undeviating justice*—it isn't punishment that's implied, but rather reassurance, as by the black box on an airplane, that whatever our course, feedback will be constant. No need to feel bad about what was thought or said or done; just learn from it and move on.

This set of affirmations became my mantra for walking, and these insights into the mysteries sustained me for years. I no longer felt limited by the short-sightedness and exclusions of my early experience with religion because now I understood that no one is excluded, the rules apply equally to everyone, and each person can choose how to experience life.

Gaps nevertheless persisted in my understanding of how to manage my life on planet earth. I still couldn't imagine, for example, manifesting a rose in my outstretched hand as I had seen a Maharishi do on The Ed Sullivan Show. So, in the mid-80s, when I heard Lazaris (a non-corporeal entity) speak, I was stimulated to learn more about the process of conscious co-creation and how it fit with my spiritual life.

Among the books presented to me at that time whose authors professed to channel non-corporeal entities were Jane Roberts' *Seth Speaks: The Eternal Validity of the Soul (A Seth Book)* and Esther Hicks' *Abraham Speaks*. I naturally jumped on board, read their books, and watched their videos because my friends were and doing so provided fodder for interesting conversation.

In 1989, feeling confined by my job—like a mouse in a small cage running the wheel faster and faster yet never getting anywhere at all—I asked for an unpaid leave of absence to reassess where I was in life and decompress from an intense three years as a federal grant writer and coordinator and first chairman of a new faculty governance system. That year off morphed into a two-year walkabout that included camping trips with Huichol Indian shamans, during which I learned about walking two paths, existing in two worlds. Each shaman is called because the animals speak to him or her. (To me, too.) They lead two lives: one as a spiritual leader, the other in the "real world" as, for example, a farmer or an artist. It reminded me of my own life as a professor in the *real world* and spiritual seeker in *my* real world.

But the biggest gift of that experience was seeing the matrix that underlies everything. My personal equivalent of the *burning bush experience*, it reaffirmed my belief that there is, in fact, "something" that ties everything together, in my experience, a sort of Primal Will-To-Good, as described in Paul Case's statement number two.

In 1990, on Vancouver Island, British Columbia, while having a cup of coffee early one morning on my friend's back porch, I suddenly, inexplicably, felt compelled to know what was happening at Kripalu Center for Yoga and Health in Lenox, Massachusetts. The next morning, flying on plastic (credit cards), I was en route to Kripalu.

There, I spent a month learning to honor every body (Kripalu Meditative Massage). So powerful was the experience that I stayed another month (Kripalu Meditative Yoga), during which I learned such other practical skills as how to focus my thoughts, to become the "Witness" who observes without interaction or judgment the sensations felt while holding a posture (and, later, events that happened around me, *off* the mat), to reach such stillness in meditation that all the world around ceases to exist, reminding me once again that I am one with All That Is.

Upon returning to Colorado, I became a yoga teacher to ensure my own practice, to continue this leg of my path. That students remarked in class on their "spiritual experience" absent any verbalization to that effect by me was reassuring. As my meditation practice deepened, I felt more and more connected and all was well . . . until LoA went viral.

As an academic and seeker, I kept my eye on this intrusion into my peace.

For those who wanted to improve their lives, I knew that "positive thinking" as taught by *Guideposts Magazine* founder Minister Normal Vincent Peale was incredibly effective. My mother had shared her copy of his book, *The Power of Positive Thinking*, when I was in high school, and it had made an impression on me. For those who wanted to improve their financial status and care, I knew that business success books like *The Secret Laws of Success* by journalist Napoleon Hill were effective. However, such works were now being supplanted by the new trend, The Law of Attraction, known by followers as LoA, popularized in the early 1970s by a group of channeled entities voiced through Esther Hicks.

My mind reduced the impact of this trend to an academic summary. *This new Law of Attraction concept combines tenets of the ancient texts with the positive thinking of New Thought Philosophy and the success movement of business, and embraces the gist of a spiritual law (the law of cause and effect, newly christened the law*

11

of attraction, or "like attracts like"), which moniker leader Hicks later employed in her book by that title, The Law of Attraction.

Some, I knew, believed Hicks' book had launched the "Law of Attraction Movement" in the 70s, but the perspective of an old gal who watched the whole thing unfold is that it didn't "go viral" until Internet came along and precipitated the release of the film, *What The Bleep?,* and, in the 90s, the Australian book and film, *The Secret.* This event, like blood in shark-infested water, fostered a feeding frenzy of writers and motivational coaches promoting wealth and success and promulgating hundreds of books, articles, courses, and workshops on "how to make millions."

None of this was part of my life, not even by way of friends or colleagues, though we continued to read some of the books and watched the films. We laughed about how everyone was talking about and practicing "how to get everything you want," but the only ones actually making any money were "those guys writing the books."

My life was busy as a full-time professor, massage therapist, yoga teacher, and psychotherapist specializing in Alchemical Hypnotherapy to help clients get past their stuck bits. That we store everything we suppress (choose not to experience) in the body and subconscious is common knowledge in those fields. I even offered personal empowerment workshops like "Healing the Inner Child," much of our "baggage," negative emotions, wounded-ness, anger, and depression, can be traced to early experiences.

Despite parents doing the very best they can, some believe that no one truly had a happy childhood simply because no *child* can every get as much as he wants. Ever met a three-year-old who didn't punctuate every utterance with "NO!"?

On a personal level, I continued my path through the 90s learning ways to heal myself like tapping meridian points using the Emotional Freedom Technique (EFT), "releasing" with the Sedona Method, and purifying myself with "decrees" of the Purple Flame of St. Germain.

That thoughts have energy and are communicated through space is a concept I learned and accepted to be true in Alchemical Hypnotherapy (1993) when I was taught how to communicate with people who were not available— whether by distance, death, or simply by personal preference —even if they lived in my house! Having had a similar experience before, that it showed up again held special meaning for me, as in, "Pay attention! This is important." I used this technique, called Etheric Plane

Communication (E.P.C.), frequently to communicate with friends, family members, and the "unavailable" woman who had become our department chair.

One evening, while thinking about a friend I hadn't seen or chatted with in perhaps three months, the phone rang. It was her. She professed to have missed talking with me and figured she'd better pick up the phone. Coincidence? I don't believe in them.

In fact, most days, despite being on the lower end of the financial bar, I was and am happier than a flock of chickadees singing to the sun on a frosty, early winter morning.

However, when The Law of Attraction went viral in the early 90s, people who had once been friends suddenly became self-appointed LoA Cops, enforcing *The Law* with everyone they knew. It happened to me twice.

The first time was when I casually mentioned that construction had begun on the vacant lot next to mine and a friend responded, "What did you do to create that?" HUH? The second time was after my best friend of seventeen years died. A concerned friend who phoned to see how I was, when I told her, said I'd feel better if I weren't so negative. Seriously? Ultimately, feeling the sting others had reported, I grew to despise the LoA and anyone who talked about it.

So, strapping on a gun-belt full of reasons, I promptly read more than twenty books about the LoA. In truth, this quest was motivated, in part, by a desire to discover something vital others had missed. Oops.

I derived considerable satisfaction from my observation that despite the deluge of media—books, recordings, films, Web sites, and blogs—proclaiming the law of attraction as an easy means to one's desire, anyone active online couldn't help but notice the confusion about its use.

What's more, that the Web site-proclaimed "leader in this field," Esther Hicks channeling Abraham, was supplementing her many books on the subject with workshops to further explain her formula, a Web site, even daily affirmations e-mailed to your computer, suggested, to me at least, that, as in the elementary school game of "gossip," many of those using LoA were missing something!

Guided by a singular voice and the varied experience accumulated on my spiritual path, I chose to do a historical evolution of the LoA concept for my metaphysics course. When my advisor changed, my intentions for the paper also changed. Even the thrill of educating a different metaphysics teacher who had spoken vehemently against the law of attraction had lost its oomph. Now I had a completely different purpose, one fueled by a burning desire to learn all I could about it.

Like the poster states: "Those who think they know are irritating to those of us who do." The raison d'etre for the little paper on LoA was to afford me the opportunity to sing the Na-Na song (in the privacy of my apartment, of course) to those who *judge their friends.*

Unknown to me at the time, of course, I was also writing the paper for myself. *Someone* believed there was something to be learned by me in this process. I know this is true. The fact that I was compelled to continue my research and writing long after the paper was accepted assured me that, for some reason unknown to me, I was most definitely writing for myself. Why else couldn't I stop?

And so, with perfect hindsight, I now regard this madness as part of my spiritual journey, and this book is offered with the intention of sharing that journey with you.

Chapter 2

The Research Stage
Guidance from the Very Beginning

Ideally, a student preparing to write a paper has a clear idea of the topic, perhaps even a thesis statement, and is looking for resources, including books and articles, which prove that thesis. I did not.

Instead, anticipating the need to write a thesis *at some point*, I read widely, anything that caught my eye that might be used in the paper I would think about later. It was during all that research that I realized my real purpose in signing up for the metaphysics course had been to give myself permission to read as widely as I chose to, to immerse myself totally in the delicious pool of metaphysics. And read I did, scarfing down books for more than six months, until suddenly I realized that the paper would be due soon, and the need to select one topic and to quit reading anything that did not apply to it became an elephant on my chest.

I stacked on the floor, sorted by category according to the list of topics acceptable in the metaphysics program, all fifty books I'd read. The stack related to the spiritual law of attraction was tallest. Contacting the school to tell my advisor, I discovered she'd moved on to another gig. Huh? Now, lacking the precious motivation of dancing academically with the advisor who had written her thesis about the LoA by choosing the same topic she had, did I really want to pursue this topic that irritated me so?

Absolutely. I still had a mission, a burning need to sing the Na-Na song.

And, as had been the case for most of my life, some other part of me was driving the bus anyway.

To gain clarity for my mission (to find the truth), I selected books not for their current popularity, but for their place in the historical evolution of the concept that people can, indeed, consciously co-create their lives by means of the spiritual law of attraction. I searched for the earliest published works I could find in such diverse areas as spirituality and religion, New Thought, and business and motivation (the latter owing to the alleged influence of metaphysical secrets on success). The fact that I had taken a similar approach in the research for my doctoral dissertation regarding why people change wasn't lost on me. Evidently, I have a need to consider different perspectives. What the different perspectives had in common this time was acknowledgement of the metaphysical perspective on thoughts attracting thoughts.

Each of the selected sources contributed elements to the Law of Attraction formulas for using one's mind to improve one's life. These formulas inevitably included mostly the same ingredients: ask for what you want, express gratitude, believe that you already have it ("act as if" and expect that outcome to be true), be aligned with Good, consciously choose positive thoughts and feelings, do the best with what you have, and allow your desire to manifest in its own perfect time.

According to Mitch Horowitz, the principle of positive thinking advocated by New Thought philosophers added to the formulas the notion of visualization: "Picture an outcome, dwell on it in your thoughts and feelings, and unseen agencies—whether metaphysical or psychological—will supposedly come to your aid."[7]

Horowitz did an amazing amount of research for his book, *One Simple Idea*, and the fact that he ordered it historically, as the evolution of "positive thinking," must have made a bigger impression than I first realized. It was one of the first books I'd read. I now see that happy coincidence as a bit of guidance I followed on this journey.

But reading wasn't the only thing I did to get at the truth. I also simply asked people about their experience with the Law of Attraction.

The Law of Attraction—How's That Working for You?

Curious about the practical application of such formulas, I surveyed a small group of self-selected participants (who already knew of, and used, the Law of Attraction) about whether they had been successful in manifesting their "dream" and what techniques they had used. I also added an open-ended question about why (they imagined) others were not successful.

The effectiveness of some of the techniques associated with the Law of Attraction as a way of accomplishing one's goals, I knew, could not be denied, the positive thinking taught by Norman Vincent Peale, for example.

I was also familiar with internationally renowned motivational speaker and minister Terry Cole-Whittaker, who teaches, using roadmaps based on her experience, how to create the life you want, and whose workshops and retreats have helped others get what they want. Having previously read *What You Think of Me Is None of My Business*, I knew I would read more of her books.

I've already explained that I chose to research LoA primarily from a historical perspective to see if I could discover from its origins and what was missing in the current formulas. Because I was meeting a requirement for a course in Western metaphysics, I steered clear of a worldwide literature review in favor only of books that presented the limited perspective of the West. I was hoping that my outcomes would differ from those recorded in other Western books on the topic. I was not disappointed, and that was fuel for the fire that bloated the thesis resulting in my choosing to write this book.

Just To Be Clear

As a former teacher, I know how important it is to define terms, whether in casual conversation, academic debate, or in the writing of a book. Therefore, please indulge me while I repeat myself: the spiritual law of attraction is, simply, "like attracts like." What it comes down to, essentially, is that thoughts have energy signatures based on associated feelings, and those thoughts are telegraphed to others. Who hasn't felt *bad vibes* in a place or from a person? From a metaphysical perspective—that is, the perspective concerned with existence, causality, or truth—whatever one routinely thinks about, believes, or does is generously matched by more of the same, sometimes a lot more! It's like placing an order to the Universal Subconscious Mind for *all other thoughts ever* that match your own. Understanding that basic concept, if that is as far as one goes, is enough to change one's life. According to U.S. Andersen, "You are what you think; you attract what you think; your life is a product of your thought and belief; and nothing in the world can change that fact."[8]

It should be noted that, throughout this book, law of attraction, in lower case, refers to the spiritual law that states that we attract "like" thoughts, people, events, and circumstances. Law of Attraction with initial caps and abbreviated LoA, refers to the currently popular "formulas for creating success and getting what you want." The modern LoA formulas typically include many, if not most, of the following elements.

- Ask for what you want.
- Express gratitude.
- Believe that you already have it.
- Be aligned with "Good."
- Focus thoughts on what you desire to experience rather than what you do not.
- Do your best with what you have.
- Allow your desire to manifest in its own perfect time.

Wanting this to be acceptable reading to anyone regardless of their spiritual path, please also note that most references to the Supreme Power will use the terms used by reviewed authors, such as Source, Universe, All That Is, Universal Mind, Universal Subconscious Mind, or Spirit. Use of a different term neither negates the All-That-Is of God, nor implies any disrespect for the All-Knowing, Omnipresent One.

I wish to state further that I am clearly, unequivocally, and unambiguously in alignment with the authors of *Life 101*, who wrote, "We're going to take a clear, unequivocal, and unambiguous position on God, religion, reincarnation, atheism, agnosticism, and all that. Our clear, unambiguous, and unequivocal position is this: We are clearly, unambiguously, and unequivocally *not* taking a position."[9]

The focus of this book is to historically explore the concepts and precepts that are the basis of LoA, and perhaps rethink the meaning of formulas developed around the law of attraction, not to define or name God. Readers are therefore encouraged to substitute their personal terms for that Supreme Power for the ones appearing here.

I also feel compelled to state that, though I've done my very best to accurately represent each work cited for its contribution to the development of LoA, you must read for yourself what each of these authors says to actually "get it." Their stories can be neither fully conveyed in, nor grasped from, paraphrasings or quotes. Would you want to be known and understood by only a paraphrased sentence or quote? That said, please see the end notes and works cited at the end of this book to further explore, at your leisure, concepts, notions, and ideas that pique your interest.

All that said, let's examine the historical origins of those elements of the LoA. The historical perspective *is* the foundation of this book, and it is, in fact, the experience that had such a whopping impact on me. I've broken up what once was single chapter to help keep the mind focused on the particular time explored.

Ready? Then turn the page.

Chapter 3

A Brief Historical Perspective #1
From the Essenes and the Bible

Expanded beyond my Master's thesis, this brief historical perspective is important to read and understand because it provides a context for the LoA. In doing so, it demonstrates LoA to be an outgrowth of what has come before rather than something new. It also clarifies some aspects of those formulas that might have impeded the user's success.

As previously stated, according to my research, the modern-day, conscious co-creation Law of Attraction process involves some or all of these things: asking for what you want, believing you'll get it, expressing feelings of already having it, being aligned with "Good," consciously focusing on what you desire to experience rather than what you do not, doing your best with what you have, and letting your desire manifest in its own perfect time. It's important to note, however, that the Law of

Attraction didn't start here, nor did it begin as a formula for getting more stuff.

The Essenes

Elements of conscious co-creation were included more than two thousand years ago in the Essene masters' answer to the question of how to maintain peace, "Three are the dwellings of the Son of Man . . . they are his body, his thoughts, and his feelings. . . . First shall the Son of man seek peace with his body. . . . Then shall the Son of man seek peace with his thoughts . . . then shall the Son of man seek peace with his own feelings."[10]

Reading this took my breath away. Already, 2500 years ago, people were being taught how to create the experience they sought, taught the power of their thoughts and feelings, and that they *lived* in a body, that they were not their body but more than their body. Seeking peace with the body from the Essene perspective is beyond the scope of this book; suffice it to say that if you are not taking good care of your earth-suit you will suffer. (More about making peace with your body can be gleaned from *The Essene Gospel of Peace, Book One: The Third Century Aramaic Manuscript and Old Slavonic Texts.*)

Relative to our search for truth about LoA, Braden asserts that the Essene formula is thought, feeling, and emotions that become the blueprint to understanding and changing the conditions of our lives. We must become the conditions of our desire from within, in our thoughts, feelings, and bodies. In other words, to bring peace we must first become peace.

Gandhi is often quoted proposing a similar perspective: "Be the change."

Every LoA formula I've encountered includes thought, feeling, and emotions, but only writers of spiritual texts mention *becoming* that which we desire.

The Bible

Jesus' efforts to teach those of his time how to preserve peace and other ways to determine their experience are recorded in Bible verses. Consider, for example, the lessons taught in Matthew. Verses one through six deal with the consequences of judging others. *Being* what you want to experience is somewhat implied in the Golden Rule, Matthew 7:12: "So whatever you wish that others would do to you, do also to them, for this is the Law and the Prophets."[11] The consequence of such behavior is understood: what you do to others is what others will do to you. We get to choose how we are treated. If we wish to be treated well, we *become* that person we wish to be by treating others well.

27

The Biblical formula for getting what you want is spelled out in Matthew 7: "Ask, and it will be given you; seek, and you will find; knock and it will be opened to you." That three hundred and fifty six verses include the word attests to "belief'" being fundamental to these prescriptions. The one that best expresses to me the importance of faith, also in Matthew 7, is: "If you have faith like a grain of mustard seed, you will say to this mountain, 'Move from here to there,' and it will move, and nothing will be impossible for you."[12]

Since the advent of the Internet and Rhonda Byrne's *The Secret*, exploring the Bible for verses relevant to LoA has been the concern of blogs, Web sites, and writers. Doron Alon, author of *The Bible and the Law of Attraction*, cites numerous Bible verses that support the Law of Attraction, Proverbs 23:7, for example: "It is through thinking that man forms that which he is." Explains Alon: "Once you change your thoughts, you will change your whole life."[13]

Alon also addresses the concerns of Christians reluctant to practice the Law of Attraction because they see it only as the pursuit of materialism: "Through Abraham, God has shown that abundance is not only his will for you, but also your birthright,"[14] and, "God has infused in all of us his essence and his creative power to have, be, and do whatever it is that we please."[15]

To further emphasize that we are intended to create as Jesus did, and that faith is key to doing so, Alon also quotes Jesus in John 14:12: "I tell you the truth, anyone who has faith in me will do what I have been doing. He will do even greater things than these."[16] Wait for it . . .

That we are not to be anxious about basic needs, but to relax knowing that our needs are already met, even as lilies and birds are cared for, is averred in Matthew 7:25-34, albeit with the proviso, in verse 33, that the kingdom of God be sought first: "But seek ye first the kingdom of God and his righteousness, and all these things will be added to you." We are cautioned that "getting more stuff" and performing miracles isn't what life on planet earth is about for us; we are here for a different purpose. According to Steven Hairfield, author of *A Metaphysical Interpretation of the Bible*, "The journey of life is only about realizing the divine and aligning with it."[17]

This seems to present a conundrum. We are told to ask and it will be given, challenged to do miracles beyond even what Jesus did, and then cautioned that it's not our main gig. Hold on; we'll return to this later in the book.

What about that *strange* verse, Matthew 25:29: "For unto every one that hath shall be given, and he shall have abundance; but from him that hath not shall be taken away even that which he hath."[18] Butterworth takes recourse to the spiritual law of attraction to explain it, stating that Jesus' statement is a metaphor meant to convey the kind of orderly law upon which the whole of the Universe is constructed. But it is Andersen who makes the meaning of that same verse crystal clear.

> Jesus spoke of the law of attraction and the habit patterns of the Conscious Mind . . . that a person who saw abundance around him was by that very act calling into existence even more abundance; and . . . a person who saw lack all about him was by that very act calling into existence an even greater lack.[19]

Suffice it to say that the current "Law of Attraction," consciously creating with thoughts, feelings, and belief, is not a new idea. In fact, besides the teachings in the *Bible* and the Essenes' position on prayer presented by Braden in *The Isaiah Effect*, early beginnings of the modern day Law of Attraction were found in the literature regarding how to be successful in the business world.

Chapter 4

A Brief Historical Perspective #2
From Business, New Thought and . . .
Switchwords!

Business

Commissioned by Andrew Carnegie to interview and
write about successful businessmen, journalist Napoleon
Hill produced one of the earliest contemporary books about
how to be successful in business that incorporates elements
of LoA. Each of the sixteen lessons in *The Law of Success*
is vital, according to Hill, because they represent what the
most powerful men in the country did to achieve success.
"This course has been created for the serious-minded
person who devotes at least a portion of his or her time to
the business of succeeding in life," wrote Hill, validating, at
least for this student, the time spent consciously co-
creating, as in prayer or visualization.[20]

Hill wrote at length about the nature and power of thought. "[The] ether is a conductor of all vibrations from sound to thought." "Every mind is both a broadcasting and a receiving station." "Every mind, or brain, is directly connected with every other brain by means of the ether. Every thought released by any brain may be instantly picked up and interpreted by all other brains that are 'en rapport' with the sending brain."[21]

If we only got this part right, understanding that our thoughts are not private, but shared with others whether we know it or not, intend it or not, imagine how different our world would be!

Hill distinguished between personal thought and intuition like this.

> There are two distinct classes of what are called Thoughts: those that we produce in ourselves by reflection and the act of thinking, and those that bolt into the mind of their own accord. I have always made it a rule to treat these voluntary visitors with civility, taking care to examine, as well as I was able, if they were entertaining; and it is from them I have acquired almost all the knowledge that I have.[22]

In my journals, I distinguish those thoughts I know are mine from those that "bolt into my consciousness" by annotating them with the word THOUGHT, all in caps. It doesn't take long to ascertain whether a thought was mine or one given me in the ongoing course of guidance.

At the end of the sixteen-lesson course, Hill reasserts the role of thought in achieving success in business.

> The power of thought has been given the dominating position throughout this course, for the reason that it belongs in that position. Man's dominating position in the world is the direct result of thought, and it must be this power that you, as an individual, will use in the attainment of success, no matter what may be your ideas of what represents success.[23]

Most likely, it was an understanding of the law of attraction that led the men interviewed by Hill to note these points of personal responsibility for success: give more than expected; align yourself with GOOD; practice tolerance and the Golden Rule; entertain positive thoughts; do your part (e.g., create a plan, determine what you'll give); and "profit from failure."

The notion that it is possible to "profit from failure" is key to maintaining a positive perspective. If we accept that no one was born knowing how to do everything right, that we are constantly learning, and view each instance in our life as a learning experience, we won't feel blown off-center when things don't go as we expect or would prefer. Staying positive, no matter what, is fundamental to success.

Hill titles the first chapter of his follow-on book, *Think and Grow Rich*, "Thoughts Are Things." He repeats that message throughout the book, emphasizing over and over the role of thought and attendant belief that success will be ours.

New Thought

In every one of the books I read on the subject (some published as early as 1900), positive thinking is deemed a critical element of success. *Thought Vibration or the Law of Attraction in the Thought World*, published in 1902 by *New Thought Journal*, for example, is focused entirely on the role, and double-edge sword nature, of thoughts in our lives. To wit: "The Universe is governed by Law—one great Law, the mighty law that draws to us the things we desire or fear, that makes or mars our lives."[24] In other words, the ability to understand and use that law affects one's sense of power over one's life.

Your Faith Is Your Fortune, published in 1941 by Neville Goddard, who published his books as Neville, was a luminary of New Thought philosophy. By comparing the process of consciously creating to the Biblical story of Joshua capturing the city of Jericho, Neville arrived at a three-step "Formula for Victory."

> 1. Define your objective, not the manner of obtaining it, but your objective; pure and simple.
>
> 2. Take your attention away from the obstacles that separate you from your objective and concentrate your thought on the objective itself.
>
> 3. Close your eyes and FEEL that you are already in the city or state you would capture; remain in this psychological state until you experience a conscious reaction of complete satisfaction in your victory. Then, by simply opening your eyes, return to your former conscious state.[25]

This formula is developed, point for point, in the preceding pages. Echoing the importance of "feelings" expressed earlier by the Essenes (Braden, *The Isaiah Effect*), Neville wrote, "Your awareness is the master magician who conjures all things by *being that which he would conjure.*"[26] In other words, as stipulated by the

Essenes, the feelings associated with the desire as already accomplished must be present.

Neville cites the Bible frequently to support his assertion that we are claiming our Divine powers, as Jesus did, by surrendering personal ego and becoming aligned with God. He explains alignment with God thus.

> Jesus, in stating that He and His Father were one but that His Father was greater than He, revealed His awareness (Father) to be one with that which He was aware of being. He found himself as Father or awareness to be greater than that which He as Jesus was aware of being. You and your conception of yourself are one. You are and always will be greater than any conception you will ever have of yourself.[27]

Now that's a mind-bender, for sure. Try it this way. I know that I am one with the Father, but the Father is greater than I am. When I am aligned with the Father, my awareness or consciousness is greater than when I am only myself. Even though I am whatever I believe I am, I am my conception of myself, in fact, I am and always will be greater than any belief or conception I will ever have of myself.

Ready for a stretch yet?

U.S. Andersen's tack is more direct; aimed at transforming one's consciousness, each chapter of his *Three Magic Words* includes carefully orchestrated arguments that build on previous arguments, followed by summary points and a meditation to anchor the point.

Like Hill and Neville, Andersen explains the magnetic and creative aspects of thought, concluding with, "Like unto like, the thing to the image, the circumstance to the vision, the answer to the prayer—on this law and this law alone are all things constructed from the atom to the solar system." He continues: "[You], by changing your thought and belief, can set up an entirely new field of magnetism, and attract those very things that you were repelling before,"[28] driving the point home with, "Every thought you entertain and accept becomes a part of you and inevitably will bring you the physical reality of your image . . . Universal Subconscious Mind awaits your choice and your belief. . . . When you truly have come to understand that there is only one mind which is every place at the same time and is in all things, you will know that the differences between you and any person on earth are purely illusory."[29]

How would it change your experience of life to know that there is only one mind and that you are a part of it, just as is everyone else?

Mine completely changed. With that discovery, that we are all part of the One, in 1989 I left my fear in a Mexican desert.

Invoking the Twenty-third Psalm—"Lo, though I walk through the valley of the shadow of death, I fear no evil, for thou art with me"—Andersen explains how we can "Let go and let God," because God is wherever we are, guiding us. "'Let go and let God'," he explains, "means to recognize that you do nothing but observe and accept, and whatever you accept is delivered to you by the Subconscious Mind."[30] Our only responsibility is to think, because our accepted thoughts are manifested in our physical world.

Truly understanding that our job is simply to choose thoughts demystifies the task of mastering thoughts. Now I can allow the parade of thoughts without feeling obligated to study them. They can simply go by like scenes in a movie or leaves blowing in the wind. Of course, if there's one I *want to experience*, I can choose it, focus on it, knowing *that will be my experience*.

Andersen formulates a definition to add clarity to the Law of Attraction phenomenon; "The law of attraction," he writes, "is the law of manifestation of beliefs and desires, and the method by which this law may be controlled so as to produce only good is by refusing to accept evil."[31]

Andersen had clarified early on, in the second chapter, what he meant by that term: "Evil is error and is illusion," that is, faulty thinking.[32]

So, besides choosing what to think and acknowledging that we are one with everything, what's our part in manifesting, according to Andersen? In the chapter headed "Intuition" he writes, "As soon as we have crystallized the thought and adopted it, we are moved by the Subconscious Mind to perform those things which will give the thought physical reality."[33] In other words, we will be guided in what we must do to achieve the physical manifestation of our desire. He later restates our role thus: "These are the tools we deal with: we think; we love; and we believe. Through thought we attain knowledge. Through love we attune ourselves with Universal Mind. Through belief we transform thoughts into things."[34]

Switchwords

Around the same time Andersen's *Three Magic Words* was published, James T. Mangan's *The Secret of Perfect Living* presented a formula for manifesting that represented an interesting departure from the crowd: the use of "one-word switches" to activate one's "subterranean machines," a.k.a., subconscious. Mangan relates his journey and how he discovered that a single word, what he calls a "switchword," could be used to affect one's experience on a variety of different concerns that keep us from "perfect living." For example, one would use the word "Change" to mitigate pain, "Reach" to find lost keys, and "Learn" to activate the "youth-saving machine," that is, to stay young.

Use of the word alone will not produce the desired result, however. One must achieve "alignment with Good." Mangan devotes half the book to helping the reader do just that, achieve "Perfect Living" status, which he defines as "a state of absolute self-togetherness, a union of the conscious and subconscious selves for the ultimate good and benefit of your whole person."[35] Switchwords, because they help to mitigate day-to-day concerns like lost keys, even finding a partner if one is lonely, make it easier to stay positive, to stay on the path of Good.

Mangan never directly states that the subconscious is the link to the All Powerful, All-Knowing God, in metaphysical circles, the Subconscious Mind. There is, nevertheless, a chapter headed "Submission to the Higher Power." It is left to readers to decide whether they are submitting their conscious mind (ego) to their own subconscious mind or to The Subconscious Mind. Specifying the target is not the issue, however; achieving alignment with one's self, bringing the conscious and subconscious mind together, is. It happens that—no surprise here—the Master Switchword for activating all processes of the body/mind is "Together."

"The theory of Perfect Living, properly practiced, can deliver a definite amount of control by the individual over his present and his future," writes Mangan. "What the world might call 'miracles' if they had been wrought by mystery, supernatural invocation, or other phenomenal means, become ordinary happenings under the aegis of Perfect Living."[36]

Mangan's switchwords were new to me and I have limited experience with them. I have, however, managed to find things ("Reach") and to relieve pain from typing with broken fingers ("Change"). Like others who complain that switchwords don't work, I suppose my success will end the instant I forget *why* they work.

When one has mastered Perfect Living, when "submission has succeeded in diminishing self-apartness and inducing a mood of inner togetherness," that is the time to test the switches on desires, distresses, and specific objectives asserts Mangan. This is done as follows.

> 1. State your want and its objective clearly and rationally, silently or aloud or both, thereby imparting to your full self

(conscious and subconscious) the exact meaning of the objective.

2. Believe in your project, in your individual role in this Perfect Living experiment. Rely totally on the processes of personal automation without attempting to know what they are. Let your body act like a sleepwalker or a subject in a semi-hypnotized state.

3.Throw the switch that sets the individual machine in motion without thinking of the meaning of the switchword, in much the same way as you would switch on a light, the vacuum cleaner, or a toaster in your home.

4. In a compliant mood of self-ductility, subjugate your reasoning process to automatic reflexes.[37]

What I believe Mangan means by the last step is that one should follow inner guidance as to what additional action to take, what some refer to as intuition, what I refer to as "guidance."

Aside from the requirement that one must master the lower self, must "align with Good," and the novel approach of using switchwords, another distinction of Mangan's plan for Perfect Living is the possibility of mitigating every niggling concern so that one realizes their "fulfillment as a

Perfect Living person, one of unified power, free of pain and fear, capable of doing anything and enjoying everything—while living in your very own glorious, self-made paradise."[38]

This is not unlike the teachings of Jesus and certain Hindu teachers. First, they emphasized, align with God (I'm using the term "Good"), then all things will be added.

What it comes down to is this. New Thought philosophers spread the ministry of accepting full responsibility for our experience by emphasizing our power to control our experience with mastery of our thoughts. They explain how the LoA works by teaching us *who we really are* (part of God/All That Is). Business author Hill explains that positive thinking fosters success by attracting resources and enables us to stay the course despite our so-called failures. Mangan's innovation is switchwords used to control our experience to achieve "Perfect Living." And all join the ancients in specifically requiring alignment with God (a.k.a. the Source of all "Good").

Then there are "those who channel dead guys."

Chapter 5

A Brief Historical Perspective #3
From Non-corporeal Beings (!)

Non-corporeal (without a body) Lazaris, a Being here to help us reach our fullest potential, has been teaching through a California man since the mid 1970s. I have seen row upon row of videos in California bookstores bearing the signature violet cover bearing the name LAZARIS in large letters on the spine. The one I bought online for this study is titled *Manifesting*.

Visualization, as it does with many other teachers, plays a central role in the approach Lazaris calls "programming techniques." Steps similar to those described for LoA are involved, but what Lazaris includes that no one else does (at least in my reading) is instruction about the Causal Plane "where cause and effect are linked to become physical reality," and the "33 Second Technique" of holding for exactly thirty-three seconds a state of extreme joy over realizing one's desire, then releasing it and not looking back. Thirty-three seconds, we are given to understand, represents the number of years Jesus lived; that amount of time is used, presumably, because Jesus was the master at manifesting.

The genesis of the process of consciously creating by means of the law of attraction, *so-named*, was a group of non-corporeals whose work is said, according to the Web site, to "have facilitated a major paradigm shift in mainstream America." Collectively called Abraham, they speak through Esther Hicks in *Abraham Speaks, The Law of Attraction, Ask and It Is Given*, and *The Vortex*, and on such recordings of live public sessions as one entitled, *Everything You Want: The Law of Attraction in Action*.

In *The Law of Attraction: The Basics of the Teachings of Abraham*, Hicks recounts three Eternal Universal Laws.

> 1. The Law of Attraction: That which is like unto itself is drawn.
> 2. The Science of Deliberate Creation: That which I give thought to and that which I believe or expect—IS.
> 3. The Law of Allowing: I am that which I am, and I am willing to allow all others to be that which they are.[39]

Reminiscent of Hill, Hicks explains, by way of emphasizing the importance of watching your thoughts, that we are all, whether we know it or not, whether conscious of doing so or not, constantly "transmitting," and that every thought is backed by emotion. Abraham offers reassurance lest the reader become tied in too big a knot worrying about the millions of thoughts cranked out each day, something to the effect, "Relax, there's this gap between your single thought and its manifestation; your single thought isn't going to manifest immediately."

At the same time, we are reminded to continuously "feel good," our job if we are to stay in the flow from Source. Abraham encourages us to seek the joy in all things, even that character who gets your back up, and to allow all to live their lives as they choose. If we are seeing the joy in all things, that is, are "allowing," then our thoughts will be positive and we'll feel good. If we focus instead on what we believe is *not* right about what we see, our thoughts will *not* be positive and we won't feel good. If we're not feeling good, it's because there's conflict between our thoughts or behaviors and our Inner Being's desire for us, and we are being alerted by our inner emotional guidance system that we are off track. In short, there are special reasons for those mantras, "If it feels good, do it" and "It's ALL good."

Note also that, in step three, "allowing," Abraham is suggesting that we rise above our petty thoughts, words, and deeds to actually live and let live without judgment. Here's the full definition of "The Art of Allowing" as it appears later in the book.

> I am that which I am and am pleased with it, joyful in it. And you are that which you are, and while it is different, perhaps, from that which I am, it is also good. . . . Because I am able to focus on that which I want, even if there are those differences between us that are dramatic, I do not suffer negative emotion because I am wise enough not to focus upon that which brings me discomfort. I have come to understand, as I am one who is practicing the *Art of Allowing,* that I have not come forth into this physical world to get everyone to follow the "truth" that I think is the truth. I have not come forth to encourage conformity or sameness—for I am wise enough to understand that in sameness, in conformity, there is not the diversity that stimulates creativity. In focusing upon bringing about conformity, I am pointed toward an ending rather than to a continuing of creation.[40]

Hicks isn't just talking about tolerating something you dislike. She is specific.

> Allowing is the art of finding a way of looking at things that still allows your connection to your Inner Being at the same time. It is achieved by selectively sifting through the data of your time-space reality and focusing upon things that feel good. It is about using your *Emotional Guidance System* to help you determine the direction of your thoughts.[41]

We are not "allowing" if we are only tolerating that guy who's not "doing it right" according to our preferences. (The friends who tell you"You're so negative" must have missed that point.) Instead, we have to find a way to deal with others while still feeling connected with good. This sounds a lot like seeing the God in all things. In any event, acknowledging that each of us is equally important in the overall scheme of this planet is a tough one for most of us.

The concept of "allowing" appears again in Step 3 of Abraham's formula, as presented by Hicks in *Ask and It Is Given*.

Step 1: (your work): You ask.

Step 2: (not your work): The answer is given.

Step 3: (your work): The answer, which has been given, must be received or allowed (you have to let it in).[42]

This certainly sounds simple enough, until you read the explanation for Step 3.

Step 3 is the application of the *Art of Allowing*. It is really the reason your guidance system exists. It is the step whereby you tune the vibrational frequency of your Being to match the vibrational frequency of your desire. . . . And we call that the *Art of Allowing*—that is, *allowing* what you are asking for. Unless you are in the receiving mode, your questions, even though they have been answered, will seem unanswered to you; your prayers will not seem to be answered, and your desires will not be fulfilled—not because your wishes have not been heard, but because your vibrations are not a match, so you are not letting them in.[43]

Had the Essenes written it, the explanation might have read: "If you are Love, your prayer will be answered; if you are still in Fear (the opposite of Love), it will not." Again, readers are admonished to be the best they can possibly be, forgiving everyone, treating everyone with love, consonant with Jesus' teachings about loving one's neighbor and the Essenes counsel about being in the emotion of Love. To put it bluntly, you won't get what you ask for, won't be "aligned with that which you desire," to use Hicks' lexicon, unless your entire life, not only your visualization time, is vibrating in alignment with Good.

Scoffers please note that in the same book, *Ask and It Is Given*, Hicks states that, "Once you become an *Allower* you will no longer attract into your experience those unwanted things, and you will experience absolute freedom and joy."[44]

Of course, there is another way to avoid unwanted things in one's experience, happily, a much simpler way, and that is to deny giving it your attention. As Neville wrote, "Just as a branch withers and dies if the sap of the vine ceases to flow towards it, so do things and qualities pass away if you take your attention from them."[45]

That might sound a lot like "tolerating." However, it's a doable first step.

Of special note in the Abraham process is the importance of "paying attention" to your feelings moment by moment, using what she calls your "Emotional

Guidance System." Otherwise, the Abraham approach to manifesting is similar to others previously discussed in that we are invited to have our desire and to spend at least ten to twenty minutes a day visualizing and feeling as if we were already experiencing it.

According to Abraham, the question of "taking action" depends on one's beliefs, as in Jesus' frequently quoted exhortation: "By your faith are ye healed." For those not quite in Lazarus mode, that is, believing so strongly you could, indeed, rise from the dead, taking personal action is probably your best bet.

Coming up next: Live Ones!

Chapter 6

A Brief Historical Perspective #4
From Live Ones!

Terry Cole-Whittaker, international motivational speaker and minister of a televised church, invoked the laws of prosperity in a different quarter, writing about activities for personal improvement. Her books *What You Think Of Me Is None Of My Business* and *How To Have More in a Have-Not World* are known to many, but most helpful for my purpose was *Every Saint Has a Past, Every Sinner, a Future* (republished as *Dare To Be Great*), in which she maps out her personal steps to success and helps readers develop their own plans. She also teaches spiritual laws, such as these ten, that she requires her students to learn.

1. The Law of Desire
2. The Law of Abundance
3. The Law of Acceptance
4. The Law of Good Fortune
5.The Law of Tithing

6. The Law of Exchange
7. The Law of Love
8. The Law of Communication
9. The Law of Appreciation
10. The Law of Investing[46]

Components of the Law of Attraction formula are included. About desire, Cole-Whittaker writes, "Any person can do great things if his or her desire is strong enough," and "Desire is the Golden Key that opens the gate to the road of personal riches."[47] She consistently pushes the reader to think big, and offers guidance with respect to the process of creating one's heart's desire via the law of attraction, faith/belief, being aligned with "Good," and through activities oriented towards "what *you* are going to do," emphasizing, as Hill did, the role of action.

Cole-Whittaker shares what she's read elsewhere to reveal what has shaped her beliefs and demonstrate that seeking to manifest dreams is not "just an American thing." From a "wonderful little book on how to manifest your dreams into reality," for example, she quotes an obscure Chinese mystic thus.

> Do your inner work first. Don't ask other people for their advice as to what you should do. First you decide what you desire to manifest. Write out the benefits you

would like to obtain, and also the specific criteria you want included in your ideal manifestation. Start with your ideal, not by looking to see what others have done or what is available, but what you really want in your heart. Begin in the future at the end result giving no attention at this time as to how or when it will happen, as this is up to God and the universe. Do not be limited by the world of appearances, what other people do or have done, or your own past experience. Work with God the Supreme, All-knowing, All-powerful and everywhere present Power of love.[48]

In the controversy regarding the level of specificity appropriate to the applications of LoA, Cole-Whittaker clearly comes down on the side of specificity, the more the better, just as Hill, in *Think and Grow Rich*, instructed readers to state precisely the amount of money wanted. It could be that the difficulty arises when what's wanted is a specific person; including someone else in your asking crosses a line. No one gets to play in another person's yard unless they're invited. Put the shoe on the other foot and see how it feels.

Regarding personal responsibility, Cole-Whittaker emphasizes, "If you want the best, you will need to *do* that which is in your ultimate best interest."[49] Prosperity conscious people do choose what's in their best interest. "Settling," accepting what isn't what you actually want, is not an example of prosperity consciousness. It is, instead, a declaration that, "This is what I deserve," and the Universe cheerfully obliges.

Cole-Whittaker says of the power of thoughts, words, beliefs, and behavior (one's consciousness in action), "Unless people willingly change their consciousness, it is business as usual. Through the magnetic quality of consciousness they will continue to draw to them the same circumstances over and over until they change their mind and behavior."[50]

This might be a good time to set the book aside and dream big. What is it you really want? Why not grab a pen and paper and list everything that would comprise your ideal life?

Cole-Whittaker identifies seven steps for manifesting one's desires.

1. **Desire the topmost**. Quoting Goethe, "Dream no small dreams for they have no power to move the hearts of men," Cole-Whittaker urges us to reach beyond our comfort zone for the very best in all things, to enlarge our vision of who we are and what we deserve.

2. Pray and ask for what you desire.

3. Seek knowledge of how to attain the ultimate. Cole-Whittaker cautions us not to wait until we're ready, until we have our "kit together," or it might never happen. She advises, instead, that we jump in: "Be afraid, if necessary, but go forward anyway."[51] Yes, action is required! "It's not our thoughts alone that create but our actions," she asserts, her "Pearl" on the topic: "Do the thing and the power is yours, but don't do it and you won't get the power."[52]

4. Do what works, and don't do what doesn't.

5. Control your mind and be positive.

6. Upgrade on a regular basis. This chapter really is about getting straight with money, asking for what you want, and other empowerment issues as well as illuminating certain spiritual laws, but Cole-Whittaker defines the title thus: "Upgrading is the process of releasing something you consider inferior and replacing it with something you consider superior."[53]

7. Keep on keeping on. Having achieved your goal, you know the steps for getting to the next one. States Cole-Whittaker: "The key is to keep on keeping on until we reach our topmost and ultimate goal and treasure."[54]

Merely glancing through these steps affords little appreciation for the teaching on which each is founded, so I explicated a bit. Like all the books here referenced, the reader will simply have to read them to get the whole story. Cole-Whittaker's books are not as simple as most LoA books. She shares a wealth of knowledge, wisdom, and experience, and does not limit her teaching to the LoA formula as presented here; she also teaches spiritual laws that govern prosperity including extreme attention to "being aligned with Good." The insights and understanding she reveals from personal experience attest to her complete and utter commitment to daring to be great.

Next in this group of "live guys" is the affable Mike Dooley, international speaker and author of *Infinite Possibilities* and *Leveraging the Universe and Engaging the Magic*. One of the panel of experts in the film, *The Secret*, Dooley forcefully asserts that "thoughts become things," and drills that message home on a daily basis into the half million plus subscribers to his "Notes from the Universe," an e-mail subscription service offered on his Web site.

Dooley emphasizes the importance of consciously focusing one's attention with thoughts, words, and deeds. "What you think, say, and do," he writes, "are your fulcrums for life's magic: the pivot points upon which the Universe and life's magic are leveraged."[55]

Dooley also emphasizes visualization, offering (on his third CD) these six guidelines.

1. Visualize once a day in a dark and quiet room.

2. Visualize no longer than five-ten minutes.

3. Put every detail in your mental image—e.g., colors, sounds, textures, and aromas, but never specific names—including extraneous ones like a passenger if you're driving your new car down the road, or a conversation, because such details make it seem more real.

4. Feel whatever you want to feel (with the attainment of this desire), because nothing impresses the Universe more than emotion.

5. Always put yourself in the picture.

6. Always dwell only on the end result—never "the cursed hows."

Dooley teaches his readers about the power of thoughts—in fact, has officially registered his trademarked slogan, "Thoughts become things. Choose the good ones!"—and (without ever mentioning it) the spiritual law of attraction. Cautioning that words are powerful, too, he warns listeners to be mindful even of casual comments, calling out, especially, those exchanged with friends, the Universe "taking your order" with each utterance of "I'm so tired" or "I just had a senior moment," assuring that you'll get more of the same.

Dooley echoes Cole-Whittaker in emphasizing the importance of "acting as if" in thoughts, words, and actions. "An act of faith suspends any contrary limiting beliefs," he asserts, explaining, "If you went to a furniture store and ordered a whole new living room suite, what would you do in the period before it arrived? Get rid of the old stuff!" Because you *know* your order will arrive as placed, you'd want that space to be clear. It's the same with anticipating to the point of expectation the fulfillment of your desire. The point is to focus on the desire and be in alignment with it through your thoughts, words, and actions.

In *Infinite Possibilities*, Dooley states that we can overcome limiting beliefs by doing two things: identify the beliefs that will serve us, and install them. If you act as if the new beliefs are already yours, the old limiting ones will fall away.

But Dooley's particular contribution to the evolution of our desire to improve our lives with conscious creating using the law of attraction is his generous sharing of his personal experience with it, especially through the live recording of his public speaking tour, *Leveraging the Universe and Engaging the Magic*. Many have written about *what to do*; Cole-Whitaker and Dooley have shown *how to do* with abundant examples from their own experience. Huge difference.

Another speaker and writer who shares her personal experience is the Reverend Edwene Gaines. Her version of conscious co-creation, presented in *The Four Spiritual Laws of Prosperity: A Simple Guide to Unlimited Abundance*, cites four laws that must all be addressed in one's pursuit of more (anything).

1. The Law of Tithing
2. The Law of Goal-Setting
3. The Law of Forgiving
4. The Law of Divine Purpose

Cole-Whittaker also embraces tithing (to your spiritual source), but Eric Butterworth, another Unity (New Thought) minister, argues that *giving* is the important issue, that tithing should be considered a baby-step towards establishing the habit or lifestyle choice of giving. With respect to the historical and biblical roots of the practice of mandatory giving, he points out that "Jesus is never quoted in support of tithing,"[56] that Jesus' teaching about the law of giving is quite specific: "Give, and it shall be given unto you"[57] (Luke 6:38). Butterworth asserts that "tithing is an excellent practice which we strongly recommend to anyone who is seeking to change his life from indigence to affluence," but explains that it is normally encouraged for all the wrong reasons, as "a gross materialization of a beautiful spiritual law"[58] (a sentiment to which I relate with respect to my feelings about the current use of the law of attraction).

Beyond Gaines' first spiritual law, her four-step process echoes Hill's approach in adding to previous models the law of circulation, that is, that there must be an exchange of some kind. In Gaines' program, the recommended exchange occurs via tithing. Her take on goal-setting is similar to Hill's, and her chapter on forgiveness amplifies earlier concepts of being aligned with Good. But it is her fourth law, Divine Purpose, that sets Gaines' work apart from others. In her final chapter she discusses the importance of commitment and finding one's divine purpose.

Like Cole-Whittaker and Dooley, Gaines illustrates each law with examples from personal experience. What is unique about her contribution is her personal resolve to "be responsible for changing the way that all people think about the potential for prosperity and abundance in their lives. . . . My mission is not complete until you, too, are living a life of true prosperity."[59]

Perhaps if more writers shared their personal experiences about how they achieved their success using their LoA formulas, more of their followers might be successful implementing those techniques.

It seemed as if something was being missed in followers' understanding. My next step was simply to ask people who had tried to consciously create something to tell me how they had gone about it. Coming up next: "The Law of Attraction: How's That Working for You?"

Chapter 7

A Little Survey

The Law of Attraction—
How's That Working for You?

To "test the wind" with respect to my thesis that there is something more to consciously creating than what popular books about LoA assert, I designed a simple ten-question survey around points of the formula I derived from the reviewed literature. I used Google docs to publish the survey online as "The Law of Attraction: How's That Working for You?"

Participants were solicited via Twitter (#LoA), Facebook, and my blog. My intent was simply to collect surveys completed by self-selected participants trolling online for such things. "Sampling" by self-selection from a target audience is acceptable in this instance, just as a study of techniques for competing in pro-tennis would solicit participants from the pro circuit but not from clubs. The survey was posted online to invite the interested, and only those familiar with LoA would even know what it was about. I also made an assumption about the level of response from social media followers; I anticipated a respectable number. ROFL! (For those who don't Tweet or Text, ROFL represents Rolling On The Floor Laughing).

When only eighteen responses were posted after two weeks, despite having well over two thousand "followers," I decided to go local (the preferred route for most things). I printed, photocopied, and hand-carried the survey to groups likely to be at least somewhat familiar with LoA even in this isolated, mountain community.

(Survey follows.)

Law of Attraction—

How's That Working for You?

1. Have you tried to create your desire by consciously using The Law of Attraction?

___Yes ___No

2. Did you create your desire? (Were your efforts successful?)

___Yes ___No

3. Which of the following approaches did you use in your efforts to create your desire? (Please check all that apply.)

___clearly stated goals or objectives
___desires stated as Positive Affirmations, e.g., "I am..."
___visualization
___emotion/feeling
___gratitude

4. If you used VISUALIZATION, how often?

___once
___once a week
___daily, until desire manifested

5. If you used VISUALIZATION, how long did you do it?

___moments
___at least 10 minutes daily
___no set amount of time and/or time varied

6. If you used intense EMOTION/FEELING, how long did you hold that feeling?

___moments
___at least 30+ seconds
___no set amount of time

7. Did you make any other changes in your routine when you were trying to create your desire with the Law of Attraction?

___Yes ___No

8. Do you believe God wants us to create using the Law of Attraction?

___Yes ___No

9. Do you believe you deserve to create your desires?

___Yes ___No

10. Why do you think some people are successful manifesting their desires using The Law of Attraction and others are not? (Brief replies, words or phrases, are good.)

***

I selected the Unitarian Church because I know some of the members and assumed a good return. However, when I asked how many copies I should bring, a representative replied "maybe ten." Half that number came back to me. Seeking more participants, I phoned the minister of the only known, regularly-meeting metaphysics group in this area, The Fellowship of Spirit, a small church in Farmington, New Mexico. I made the hour drive with an envelope stuffed with surveys. Twenty-three of the twenty-five adults in attendance completed the survey. Twenty-eight of the manually distributed surveys were returned, ten more than online (local *is* better), giving me forty-six completed surveys.

The survey was introduced, whether online or in person, with the request: "If you've ever used the Law of Attraction to consciously create your desire, then please complete this survey." Because the survey was designed for those who had tried, at least once, to co-create using the Law of Attraction, those who accepted were reminded again, in the first question, of the target group: "Have you tried to create your desire by consciously using The Law of Attraction?"

Responses to all but the concluding open-ended question were hand-tallied on a master list and converted to percentages. Responses to that last question—"Why do you think some people are successful manifesting their desires using the Law of Attraction and others are not?"—were categorized and their frequency tallied.

Responses to all but the last question on the survey are discussed below, responses to the latter presented in Chapter 8.

Limitations. There are, admittedly, limitations to this study. Using the Internet, especially Twitter, to collect self-selected participants' responses to a survey is a valid technique, presuming a respectable response rate is not.

Had I not assumed, I might have made the effort to identify more target groups within driving distance, say, the eight-hour drive over several scary mountain passes to Denver.

Two of the forty-six participants complained about the lack of a "sometimes" response for individual survey questions. Had I had been in their shoes, I certainly would have agreed! But the omission was intentional, meant to force respondents to admit that they either *are* or *are not* doing THAT (whatever the question was about). On reflection, perhaps including a "generally" response might have mitigated this concern.

However simplistic in nature, the survey proved to be more than a mere "test of the atmosphere." Remarks of participants as they turned in their surveys in the Farmington church warmed my heart and boosted to the commitment level my already fervent interest in this topic. Most commented that they expected their practice to improve simply by virtue of what they had been exposed to in the survey items. Charmed by their interest, I committed to do my best to answer the questions they raised!

Results of the Survey

Survey items are referenced parenthetically (e.g., item number one as (#1)), but the question content is included with each statement to avoid the need to refer back.

That 84 percent reported that they had, indeed, tried to consciously create their desire using the Law of Attraction (#1), but only 70 percent that they had been successful (#2), suggests some misunderstanding or misapplication of the process, at least in terms of the techniques itemized in the third survey item.

Comparing the approaches they used (#3) against a list derived from the literature, fewer than two-thirds selected "clearly stated goals or objectives," which are fundamental to formulas for "getting what you want" (e.g., Hill, Cole-Whitaker, Mangan, and Gaines), and "Positive Affirmations (#3), to express desires, e.g., 'I am... '," which is specified or implied by most writers (especially Andersen and Neville).

At least two-thirds reported using visualization, emotion/feeling, and gratitude, but only 46 percent used visualization "daily, until desire manifested" (#4), and 72 percent indicated that the time invested in visualization varied (#5).

The use of emotion/feeling, deemed a critical component in the Essenes (Braden, *The Isaiah Effect*) and by Lazaris, Hicks, and Dooley, was reported by only 72 percent (#3), of whom 20 percent indicated that they held the feeling for "at least 30 seconds" (in line with Lazaris'

33-second technique) and 57 percent for "no set amount of time" (#6), suggesting that the expression of emotion and/or feeling was, indeed, viewed as part of the process, but perhaps not as *that* big a deal.

"Did you make any other changes in your routine when you were trying to create your desire with the Law of Attraction?" (#7) was an attempt to discover how many believe they have to do something besides "visualize with feeling" to get what they want. The literature is of two minds about "taking action," (1) you do your part/are guided to do your part (e.g., Dooley, Doran, Andersen, Mangan, Cole-Whittaker, and Gaines), and (2) action is not required if your belief is strong enough (Jesus and Hicks). Respondents were almost evenly split: 52 percent reporting "Yes," 48 percent "No," regarding making any other changes in their routine when using the Law of Attraction.

All components of the process except "taking action" being included in a previous question (#3), this was admittedly a bit of a trick question. Anyone truly familiar with the process as described by the authors reviewed in this study would, however, at the very least, have made the "positive thinking" change, in other words, would have become more aware of the power of their thoughts and made changes to act on that understanding beyond the moments they spent visualizing.

Another trick question (#8) was intended to reveal how many people regarded God as "Morgan Freeman in a white suit in that office up in the sky" (respectful nod to the 2003 movie, *Bruce Almighty*) versus God as the Universal Mind, Subconscious Mind, All-That-Is that everything living or not is made of, or *even their own subconscious* (Mangan). Success with the Law of Attraction does, in fact, seem to depend upon how one understands and relates to one's "God," whether that God is, well, GOD, or merely energy to be manipulated, as defined by one respondent.

Recall that 70 percent of respondents reported success using the LoA. Moreover, 76 percent responded "Yes" to "Do you believe God wants us to create using the Law of Attraction?" (#8).

The happiest response on the survey was to the question, "Do you believe you deserve to create your desires?" That 91 percent checked "Yes" suggests healthy self-esteem and/or a healthy understanding of and relationship to the concept of God.

Most enlightening, however, at least for me, was the response to the open-ended question, "Why do you think some people are successful manifesting their desires using the Law of Attraction and others are not?" (#10).

Responses to that question, grouped by category and italicized, are reported in the following chapter, supplemented with quotes from the sources reviewed in previous chapters.

Chapter 8

Understanding Why We Fail
Answers from the Authors of My Sources

Grouped into categories, responses about why we fail in our application of The Law of Attraction might be helpful as a sort of self-check. For example, reading through the discussions following each response, one might ask, "Am I doing this?" Each set of statements is accompanied, for purposes of clarification, by information and quotes from the authors of my sources.

General Remarks about the Process of Conscious Creating

Successful manifesting serves others and the greater good; unsuccessful serves the flesh—me, me, me.

Whether one must create only to serve others or it's okay to pile up physical things for oneself is a touchy subject. One respondent stated outright "evil people manifest as easily as good ones." This isn't something I choose to address, and, truthfully, I found nothing specifically about this topic in the resources I consulted. Coincidentally, the following e-mail from the Hicks' Web site arrived the morning I was writing this chapter: "The Universe is not discriminating about the rightness or the wrongness of your request. It is here to accommodate all requests. All you have to do is be a Vibrational Match to your request, and the Universe will yield it to you" (Abraham, Esther, and Jerry Hicks, excerpted from the workshop: Sacramento, CA on May 13, 2000). Seemingly, at least according to Hicks, LoA works for anyone who consistently aligns with whatever it is they desire.

Clear Intentions

Being very clear with visioning and intentions. Being very certain of what you desire.

The jury's out on this one, because it has always been controversial, whether one is talking about prayer or creating. Some advocate specificity, the more, the better; others insist we should focus on the qualities we seek and let the Universe choose for us. My recommendation would be to experiment with both and see what works.

The authors considered this, too. Hill was definite about specificity; to create your desire, he wrote, "fix your heart and hand on a definite, well-conceived purpose."[60] Hill's steps to create wealth, in Think and Grow Rich, are even more precise.

1. Fix in your mind the exact amount of money you desire.

2. Determine exactly what you intend to *give* in return for the money you desire—i.e., there's no such thing as a free lunch.

3. Establish a definite date when you intend to *possess* the money you desire.

4. Create a definite plan for carrying out your desire, and begin *at once*, whether you are ready or not, to put this plan in action.

5. Write out a clear, concise statement of the amount of money you intend to acquire, name the time limit for its acquisition, state what you intend to give in return for the money, and describe clearly the plan through which you intend to accumulate it.

6. Read your written statement aloud twice daily, once just before retiring at night, and once after arising in the morning. As you read—see and feel and believe yourself already in possession of the money.[61]

Andersen seems to agree with Hill, describing one who successfully manifests as one who makes each decision clearly and without contradiction and holds to it with complete confidence until it has arrived. Perhaps that "complete confidence" is what Hicks means when she writes that one must be in Vibrational Alignment with that which is desired. Andersen also cautioned against being wishy-washy.

> He will know of his Father's tireless energy and unbounded goodwill, but he will respectfully refuse to tax them by contradicting himself or by vacillating. He will not, for example, say "I am going to be successful," and then a few hours or days later say, "I am not going to be successful." He will not say "do, don't, start, stop, give, withhold."[62]

Mangan, too, is adamant, asserting that before we even attempt to practice creating, we must first be "together," both our conscious and subconscious selves brought together on the same side, as it were. "Self-togetherness is the very best first goal you can set for yourself, " Mangan writes. "To accept it as your first goal is pure belief. With enough reflection the two sides of you find it easy to accept, as the best thing in life."[63] He might have learned this from Andersen, who earlier wrote, "Men and women of genius are those in whom there is a perfect balance between the Subconscious Mind and the Conscious Mind. It is balance we strive for, balance between the great creative power of the Universal Subconscious Mind and the Conscious Mind."[64]

Think about it for a moment. Haven't you ever been "of two minds" about something? Part of you wants to get involved with a committed relationship; the other part doesn't and will sabotage that desire in a heartbeat. Maybe you think you want a bigger house or more money, and then you realize how it will change your life, so you abandon that desire.

In my experience, lack of commitment or alignment shows up when I put something on Craig's List and it doesn't sell. Why? Because I'm having second thoughts about it. That old recliner I bought for shoulder surgery takes up half my tiny living room, reducing the space I have for yoga, but it also happens to be the best darn reading chair I've ever had, and the reader part of me is reluctant to let it go. Internal conflict about what is wanted guarantees failure. We say, "Oh, guess it wasn't meant to be," as if we were not responsible.

Mangan insists that one should ensure that everyone (conscious, subconscious) is on board with a desire, that this is critical to bringing about change. He suggests having a little chat with your subconscious when you intend to make a drastic change like dieting or giving up tobacco or alcohol (or selling a beloved, ratty, reading chair!).

One of the most used processes back in my Alchemical Hypnotherapy day was the "Conference Room," wherein any sub-personality that had an opinion about a client's desire was invited to to take a seat at a large conference table. All were interviewed for their stances and deals struck to get everyone on board with the pending change. That process eliminated a lot of the sabotaging by clients of "mixed minds" about something as important as a career change or termination of a love relationship.

But what if you're not sure what you want to be, have, or do? Mike Dooley, sharing from his own experience in *Leveraging the Universe*, says, "If you don't know where you want to go, start going somewhere—anywhere!" (CD#4). While you're "out there" doing whatever it is you enjoy doing, having fun, feeling good, the Universe is bringing you more and more similar situations, people, circumstances, so you can keep on having those good feelings. The point is that you have to be "out there" doing something for serendipity to occur. As Theodore Roosevelt said, "Do what you can with what you have, with where you are."[65]

Finally, if nothing else has worked, we can always, according to Hicks, have the goal, "I want to know what I want." She explains how that works to clarify your desire.

> As you begin saying, I want to know what I want," you will begin to attract, by Law, all sorts of examples. And as you are collecting the data that comes to you, let your dominant intent, in each day, be to look for things that you want. Then you can look around you and see in others those traits or characteristics that you would like to have in your own mate or companion or work.[66]

Thoughts, Hidden Beliefs, and Feelings

One's experiences, situation, and environment are reflections of one's inner thinking, feeling, and attitudes. The outer reflects the inner. That is why paying attention to one's thoughts and emotions is so important.

Attracting the negative—(e.g., thinking about getting out of debt rather than generating abundance).

Thinking without feeling. Thoughts don't become things. What you feel about the thought does. Emotion is the fuel behind the transformation.

Intensity of desire.

Thoughts

Of all the elements of LoA, thought interested me most. Among my sources, Atkinson was the first (1902) to point out the need to fully understand the value of thoughts.

> We often hear repeated the well-known Mental Science statement, "Thoughts are Things," and we say these words over without consciously realizing just what is the meaning of the statement. If we fully comprehended the truth of the statement and the natural consequences of the truth back of it, we should understand many things that have appeared dark to us, and would be able to use the wonderful power, Thought Force, just as we use any other manifestation of Energy.[67]

The general way of using that power is to focus your thought on what you desire to experience rather than what you do not. It seems simple enough, but it's not only during visualization or prayer that positive thinking is required.

Perhaps those practicing LoA miss that point. Andersen is quite clear about how thoughts work.

> The law of attraction is neither more nor less than the law of attracting thoughts, and a process of choice does it. Whatever you choose to think is sent to you from the limitless reaches of universal intelligence. These thoughts, once having been accepted by you, will manifest in the physical world.[68]

Of all the books I've read on the subject, none was so helpful in clarifying this amazing concept as Andersen's *Three Magic Words*. In fact, I've been working with my copy for several months now and am beginning to embrace I AM more than ever as a result.

Clarifying the importance of the spiritual law of attraction in the process, Cole-Whittaker writes: "Unless people willingly change their consciousness, it is business as usual. Through the magnetic quality of consciousness they will continue to draw to them the same circumstances over and over until they change their mind and behavior."[69] She seems to be saying that it's not only when we're sitting in meditation or visualizing that thoughts are important, but *every moment that we're awake.*

Like Hill, Cole-Whittaker asserts that "Through the law of attraction we can draw to ourselves the most desirable people, things, and circumstances by creating the right mentality, force-field, and mental equivalents."[70] Echoing Andersen's assertion that we choose which thoughts to have and which to accept, she later states, "By creating a mental shield of discernment, we are able to accept the favorable and reject the unfavorable."[71]

Alon adds that, "Man moves in a world that is nothing more or less than his consciousness objectified. . . . The world is the mirror magnifying all that I AM conscious of being."[72] In other words, what you see in others is a product of your own thoughts and beliefs. Alon is certainly not the first one to articulate this. You'll also find it in *The Isaiah Effect*, when Braden discusses what he learned from the Essenes–that what we see around us merely mirrors our thoughts and beliefs within ourselves, what about us needs to be healed.

It's a lesson we need to absorb and share. When we judge others, we are, in fact, only pointing fingers at ourselves.

Alon also cautions about governing that which you choose to accept from others as part of your reality. "A man must discipline himself," he writes, "to hear only that which he wants to hear, regardless of rumors or the evidence of his senses to the contrary."[73]

Neville takes thought to the limit with his assertion that daydreaming and wishful thinking won't do, that you must "Claim yourself to be the thing desired. I AM that!"[74]

Plainly, a sense of abundance depends on understanding how positive thinking attracts what is wanted, and such understanding must also include how the Power that shoots those attracted thoughts back is perceived.

My two cents? Science tells us that thoughts are things and that the universe consists of something that is in everything including space. Some survey respondents called the force that handles the attraction part of the LoA formula as "merely energy," presumably the energy of the thoughts themselves. Wouldn't that energy need to be in some kind of substance that pervades everything for that to work? And if that's true, perhaps, like metaphysicians, people who say "it's only energy" also use terms like Universe and Universal Mind to define that "something."

If, on the other hand, you believe in God and God's omnipresence, that there is nowhere God is not, then you must also believe that you are part of God. If you do, then you must also believe that to be true of all others, that you are one with All That Ever Was or Ever Will Be. If everyone is in God and God is in everyone, then sharing happens. When you have a thought, others get it, too.

Both views seem to support the notion that we're all in the same soup. Hence, the term the Universal Subconscious Mind, which indicates that my little subconscious mind, like all others, is part of the bigger one. When a thought occurs and I choose it (give it my attention), I'm signaling to the All-That-Is that I want more just like that one, to which Universal Subconscious Mind replies, "Sure! Here's fifty bazillion just like yours from all thoughts that were ever thought." (Just thinking out loud.)

Hidden Beliefs

One respondent wrote that people are *unsuccessful due to old negative thought patterns or negative feelings and beliefs,* and many of the popular books on LoA are happy to join their readers in the belief that "I can't . . . because I have this old stuff in my head."

Most of my clients, when I was an Alchemical Hypnotherapist in the 90s, were seeking to change their experience by digging around in their subconscious. It definitely worked, one issue at a time. It's relatively quick, a few sessions versus years with traditional therapy. Even so, there's a more direct path one can take: control your mind, choose your thoughts, and plant new beliefs in your subconscious with positive affirmations.

Andersen assures those bogged down by whatever might lurk in their subconscious that it can be overcome by positive thoughts. Hear that again: positive thoughts overcome those nasty negative ones buried in your subconscious. Andersen calls them "Prompters." "Happily," he states, "you can remove each of these insidious Prompters yourself. What's more, you can, by understanding the laws and dynamics of life, remove the cause of them, so that they will plague you no more. . . . Nothing is impossible in the mind of man, for the Conscious Mind controls the Subconscious Mind and the Subconscious Mind is all-powerful."[75]

In other words, you don't need to go looking for what's buried in your past, those old beliefs you formed as a child or developing adult. Simply embrace, now, that you are THAT, and you are.

Andersen states that, "We need not remove these negative prompters as an especial procedure. Since positive will override negative, all that is necessary is for us to install in the Subconscious a group of positive Prompters. The existence of these will dissipate all negative Prompters and allow the individual to expand to the full blossom of his power."[76]

Instilling positive Prompters involves using affirmations and consciously choosing thoughts. In my experience, the best times for using affirmations are before you get out of bed, during physical exercise, and just before nodding off to sleep.

Finally, remember that Dooley addressed this issue earlier, explaining, in *Infinite Possibilities*, that we can overcome limiting beliefs by doing two things, (1) identifying the beliefs that will serve us, and (2) beginning to install them. In other words, act as if the new ones are already yours and the old limiting beliefs will fall away.

Feelings

"When thought, feeling, and emotion are not aligned," Braden writes, "each may be considered as out of phase with the others . . . [and] the result is a scattering of energy."[77] It is noteworthy that the Essenes distinguished between "emotion" and "feelings," asserting that "they must first be considered independently, then merged into a union of feeling that becomes the silent language of creation."[78] Emotion is the "source of power." There are two emotions, love and whatever is believed to be its opposite, often described as fear. (As an aside, *A Course in*

Miracles posits Love and Fear as the two choices for the driving force of one's life.)

[Are you mostly happy or mostly fearful? Mostly happy people see love all around them. Mostly fearful people see danger everywhere. Think about it.]

Feeling is asserted by Braden to be the key to prayer because "it is our feeling world to which creation responds."[79] He explains that thought and emotion come first, then feeling. Whenever we say something like we need more, fear is generally the emotion driving those statements. The feelings generated by such a statement— we 'need more'— are the feelings that create the outcome. Consider consider this: if every time we think of money, we feel bad, then what do you suppose the outcome will be? "How are we to create money . . . if the feelings that empower our creation are "crummy" and "yuck"?"[80]

A perfect example of appropriate use of feeling when expressing one's desire is illustrated in Braden's story of a Native American praying for rain.

> I began to have the feeling of what rain feels like. I felt the feeling of rain upon my body. Standing in the stone circle, I imagined that I was in the plaza of our village, barefoot in the rain. I felt the feeling of wet earth oozing between my naked toes.

I smelled the smell of rain on the straw-and-mud walls of our village after the storms. I felt what it feels like to walk through fields of corn growing up to my chest because the rains have been so plentiful. . . . We must first have the feelings of what we wish to experience . . . [and] from that point forward . . . our prayer becomes a prayer of thanks . . . for the opportunity to choose which creation we experience.[81]

I love that quote because it exemplifies Neville's notion of "becoming that" better than anything I've come across, and following his example in my prayers has made a huge difference.

Perhaps some present-moment practice is worth considering. For example, next time you feel really happy, notice some sensory details you can recall when you *don't* feel that way.

Belief and Faith

People who can visualize and believe it can be possible do the things necessary to make it happen; those with no faith do not.

Underlying beliefs and social negatives can get in the way. And some probably don't believe it works, so when it fails, they're right . . . for themselves.

90

Those who are successful experience success with removing judgment/belief conflicts.

I do better just by asking and letting go immediately and then the Universe works so fast that it's amazing.

An uncertainty about their belief system.

Belief. If it's a law, then the only explanation of failure is a misapplication of the law. If it is a belief, there are many competing beliefs that could sabotage it.

By having faith. They don't let go of the end result and get attached to the outcome. The key is to let it go and trust the Universe with your desires.

One must believe that God permeates all that is, then believe and act on that belief.

Judging from the number of comments, belief might just be the greatest challenge to manifesting, yet its importance is underestimated. Jesus probably said it best: "Truly, if you have faith and don't doubt, you can do things like this and much more. You can even say to this Mount of Olives, 'Move over into the ocean,' and it will. You can get anything—anything you ask for in prayer—if you believe."[82]

Sadly, most of us simply aren't there yet. Cole-Whittaker distinguishes two kinds of faith: blind faith and faith backed by experience. "Obviously," she writes, "we need to begin with blind faith. Faith by direct experience will come as we witness the results of our prayers and supplications."[83]

It takes practice. Neville likens the process of adjusting our belief to getting used to wearing a new garment; we're always checking to see how it fits. In other words, when we quit asking "is it here yet?" we will have developed faith. Ultimately, Neville dares us to claim that I AM (that), to become whatever it is we desire with such intensity that it is already done, much as in Braden's recounting of the role of feeling in the prayer for rain.

Alon, on the matter of emphasizing that we must believe we already have it, cites Mark 11:24: "What things soever ye desire, when ye pray, believe that ye receive them, and ye shall have them."[84]

Gratitude

Interesting to me is that no respondent commented on gratitude. Not a single one! Reckon this gives me license to wax about it for a while.

Most modern writers (whom I did not include in my study) include gratitude as a sort of add-on, something to do each day. My understanding, however, is that gratitude is a way of life. To attract abundance, we must see abundance around us at all times. The sky is full of stars; trees are full of leaves; the ocean is full of drops of water; there are bazillions of grains of sand. If we can immerse ourselves in the feeling of abundance that comes with contemplating endless stars, leaves, drops, or grains, we can experience the feeling of abundance. Only when we begin to feel that we are surrounded by abundance can we imagine that there's enough for everyone (a concern some people have expressed, one which I personally believed for years).

Andersen explains, regarding that Bible quote that inevitably seems to stump people—the passage about the one who hath and the one who hath not—that the wealthy habitually "think wealthy" and the poor habitually think "poor." Those who see and *expect* abundance all around them tend to think wealthy and be wealthy.

Expressing gratitude now for everything we have, everything we see around us, can help alter the "poor" perspective. It's worth trying just to notice the difference. In 1991, when I first heard the label, "hair shirt mentality," applied to me, *coincidentally* I had to think a long time to come up with twenty things for my new, daily "gratitude ritual." Now, more than twenty years later, I easily find reasons to be grateful all day long. It just takes practice.

The need for gratitude is included in every source cited herein. The perspective in Braden's paraphrase of the observations of the Native American about his rain prayer is that gratitude is part of the prayer. "Our prayer," Braden writes, "becomes a prayer of *thanks* for the opportunity to choose which creation we experience. Through our thanks, we honor all possibilities and bring the ones we choose into existence."[85]

One idea you could do right now is to set the book down and grab your journal for a little gratitude. Start listing everything you ever wanted. Add the day you received it with the words, "I received this, with gratitude, on ___." On my list were things like a two-wheel bicycle, a puppy, and, fast-forwarding about twenty years, "a passing grade on the language proficiency part of the doctoral exams" and . . .. (Yikes!) Pages and pages listed the abundance I'd already experienced. The immense feeling of gratitude I felt from that simple exercise made me realize, once more, that I have led an abundant life in which the Universe/God has always watched over me, even to the point of answering my guarded, secret desires.

Doing Your Part

The LoA is far too simplistic. Manifesting anything takes our own active participation and effort, not just sitting around looking at Vision Boards.

On the question of taking action, Alon states, "Although the goal may simply manifest with little or no action on your part, often you will find that God will nudge you to take the actions required."[86] In my experience, manifesting parking spots near the entrance to my destination is an example of "little or no action on your part." I simply state silently that I have one and expect it to be there when I arrive, and it always is. An elderly friend calls me "The Parking Spot Goddess."

Hill, on the other hand, is insistent that one not only must take action, but must do the best one can with what one has. In other words, don't waste time waiting for the perfect set-up to start working towards your desire. He also encouraged the habit of doing more than required, especially if seeking a different job, explaining that even when you hate your job you must master it before you'll be given the opportunity to move, which reasoning echoes the spiritual law that one who is positive is a magnet for positive experience.

Cole-Whittaker asserts that we must "act as if" we have already achieved our desire. "In essence," she writes, "develop the attitudes, habits, and actions that are appropriate for who and what you desire to be, and you will be able to achieve your goals and live your dreams."[87] She also has detailed action plans indicating that our part is to discover what it takes to get the job done, perhaps from others who have done it, then to do whatever we can. Gaines does, too, but hers are more about "how must I change" instead of "what must I do."

Most outspoken about the need to take action is Mike Dooley, who, in the second CD of *Leveraging the Universe and Engaging the Magic*, explains by means of his triangle diagram his concept of roles related to creating a desire. The goal is at the pinnacle, from which a straight line down to the base divides the effort into what you can do and what the Universe does. The left side is your part, "not the 'cursed hows' but the things you're doing 'to get the Universe into the game'," for example, visualizing every day, studying your beliefs, making cold calls, what Dooley calls "pitching balls to the Universe."

Acknowledging that sometimes the action is asking questions and sometimes it's "just clearing your plate," he nevertheless insists that you keep doing something, whether you see the relationship to your goal or not. He frequently quotes former president Theodore Roosevelt's "Do the best you can with what you have." He cites personal examples of doing all kinds of seemingly unrelated things just to have something to do, then he shows how doing all that seemingly unrelated stuff was ultimately required to get where he wanted to be. In his parlance, the Universe used all those efforts to take him to where he is now: an international speaker with best-selling books.

The point is this: you don't have to know what you want. You only need to keep busy doing things you enjoy, you might enjoy, you might at one time have enjoyed. As Dooley would say, pitch balls to bring the Universe into the game so the magic can happen.

Allowing

Not allowing enough time.

Some things have manifested, some just didn't happen—as of yet.

Hill includes in his Laws of Success "profit from failure," that is, learn from your mistakes, because all too often we assume when our expectation isn't immediately realized that we have failed instead of recognizing what appeared to be failure as simply the thing that had to

---

happen next to take us another step closer to the outcome sought. Neville says that because we do not understand that our consciousness is forever out-picturing itself in conditions around us, we keep checking to see if our desire has come yet, when what is required is absolute conviction.

Bottom line: Sometimes the thing happens immediately, sometimes it takes longer, and sometimes the Universe requires us to go through extra steps that bring about all the required circumstances for the thing to happen.

[Note: Because the participants clearly viewed Hicks' concept of "allowing" as a time of waiting, allowing the thoughts to take form, I chose compatible replies from the sources used. However, that is not my understanding of Abraham's message expressed via Hicks as stated in Chapter 2. Still, this section is based on participant comments, so I'm rolling with it!]

Alignment with Spirit/God/Universe...

I think once someone comes into alignment with the energy of Spirit, He opens up "the way;" however, I do believe that despots use this same power, as there is no more duality and it works both ways.

Braden observes that the "Essene masters viewed our body as a convergence point through which the forces of creation join to express the will of God." "[It] is within the experience of time and space," he elaborates, "that spirit works through matter."[88] For this reason, successful creation must involve alignment with Source; Braden cites Mark 12:30: "Thou shalt love thy God with all thy heart, with all thy soul, with all thy mind, with all thy strength." "To focus our prayer," he clarifies, "we must love the creative principle of life itself, our Creator, with all our heart, soul, mind, and strength. Because we are one with our Father in heaven, in doing so, we have just loved ourselves."[89]

The need to be connected with Source/Creator or whatever name one uses for God is repeated by Andersen, Butterworth, Cole-Whittaker, Neville, even by Hicks. In fact, according to Neville,

> Man fails to do the works of Jesus Christ because he attempts to accomplish them from his present level of consciousness. You will never transcend your present accomplishments through sacrifice and struggle. Your present level of consciousness will only be transcended as you drop the present state and rise to a higher level.[90]

Andersen cautions against imagining that you are the one doing it. "[The] truth," he writes, "is that 'I' does nothing but choose and accept and all things are done by the Universal Subconscious Mind."[91] He further declares that:

> As long as a man carries with him a sense of having to do anything all by himself, he will inevitably fail at what he attempts to do. But when he . . . sees his unity with all life and all things, rejects personal isolation, then he invites the great power into his life, and all things are arranged according to the good he desires.[92]

Mangan invites readers to choose whether they want to submit to their own subconscious mind or to THE Subconscious Mind (a.k.a. God), at the same time insisting that submission to a higher power is required, even to use his one-word switches! In his chapter on the subject, Mangan offers gentle arguments for egos that imagine they are the supreme power in their lives, beginning with his delicious description of putting oneself in the hands of a shoeshine boy. It's not always, he observes, for the shoes that we seek such services, but the relief of burden, of giving oneself over to another. Writes Mangan:

It does not matter what that Something Bigger is. It does not matter to what or to whom we submit, just so long as we do submit—without bitterness, without odious comparisons. Submission never takes away an ounce of your integrity. Every day you submit to the law of gravity, the passing of time, the conventions of society, of law and order. Yet you find no thrill in doing what you must do, the things that are denied the choice of not doing. But doing what you do not have to do, giving up what you do not have to give up, always makes you a bigger and better person.[93]

The essence of Mangan's message is that what needs to be created is "togetherness," of conscious and subconscious, *the dueling souls within* (he frequently quotes Goethe: "There are two souls in my own breast, and one is determined to beat down the other"). Mangan repeatedly states that one must be able to release conscious control to access the limitless world of the subconscious, and he doesn't care if it's spelled with a little "s" or a big one!

From my perspective, having studied the historical evolution the LoA and listened to people practicing with it, a single red flag waves for attention. The outstanding cause for failure in efforts to consciously create using the law of attraction appears to be related to the issue of our alignment with Good/God/Source, whether it shows up as poor self-esteem, feeling unworthy, inability to experience gratitude, being challenged by the need to have positive thoughts and feelings, or being able to sustain faith and belief that our prayer will be answered. The Essenes wrote about being aligned with the emotion of Good. Hicks writes about "allowing" and using our Emotional Guidance System to stay in the flow with Source. All New Thought writers stress positive thinking. Perhaps it's time to look at ways we can feel Good more of the time.

Chapter 9

Ways to Stay Connected:
Simple Techniques to Feel Good More of
the Time

The Law of Attraction is presented as an opportunity
for people to participate consciously in the creation of their
lives. The notion that our thoughts, words, and deeds could
have so much power—especially that our thoughts,
repeated with feeling, act like a magnet to draw to us ideas,
circumstances, people, and events—can be overwhelming.
Yet the formulas are remarkably simple. At least that's
what we're told by those who have made readily available
to anyone, anytime, anywhere, what heretofore was known
only to those who studied ancient texts or metaphysics.

Unfortunately, abundant confusion about the process is
manifested in its frequent failure. There are so many
variables associated with the popularized version of the
Law of Attraction, which generally is believed to be a

single formula consisting only of a few steps, that mastering one thing at a time might be a better way to start. Alternatively, one might attempt to determine where the weakness lies and do whatever is necessary to mitigate it. Consider taking the survey reproduced in Chapter 7. As with so many things, the problem could be operator-error.

Experience with colleagues and thousands of students in an academic context suggests to me that humans are fundamentally challenged by the need to master their thoughts, stay positive, and feel worthy. We are challenged, in other words, by the need to align with Good. If that's true for you, the following techniques have been observed to yield rather immediate success.

1. **Accept responsibility for your experience**. The spiritual law of attraction demands as a first step that we accept responsibility for our experience. Were we to work consciously only with this one principle, and accept full responsibility for everything we experience throughout each and every day, our lives would change immeasurably. In the sense that doing so eliminates the option to place blame, to feel helpless or angry about one's situation, accepting responsibility for one's actions is empowering.

Learning to own mistakes and voice them is part of the deal. I learned about owning my mistakes from a colleague when I first started teaching at the local college in 1976. The team of professors had a planned meeting immediately after the morning class where unpleasant business would be handled: failing a student from the block program! I was teaching the class on that particular day, and allowed myself to get caught up with students' questions afterwards, thinking "Surely they'll understand; surely students are more important." I was mistaken.

My favorite professor in the department came to get me and invited me to his office, where he explained what I had agreed to do (attend the meeting immediately after class) and spelled out the effect my absence had had on my colleagues (made them shoulder the unpleasant duty when it should have been all three of us). I can't say it felt good to be caught being bad, but I certainly got it, and my experience of life, generally, has been much more positive since.

Learning to accept responsibility for one's experience, whether in thought or verbally, is prerequisite to an empowered life.

In the 1980s, not long after the experience recounted above, I stumbled across Peggy Dylan Burkan's book,

Guiding Yourself Into A Spiritual Reality: Workbook. The Introduction is subtitled, "Are you playing the game yet?" "The Game," we learn in the first sentence, "is simply to use your creative mind to make your life more fun, playful, fulfilling, conscious and joyous."[94] Isn't that what most people expect from LoA? Burkan's workbook is not only informative; it's fun to use and it guides readers every step of the way.

2. Clear the negatives. Burkan includes a process for clearing negatives. The reader is invited to look at every choice he's made in the light of enhancing self-love, because love is the objective of personal growth. "Clearing these negatives out happens," she explains, "by your willingness to be aware of them, experience any attached emotion, and change them."[95]

Recall that from the Essenes to *A Course in Miracles,* the consensus is that we're driven by only two emotions, Love and Fear, the latter defined as anything that is not Love. "You have the ability," Burkan asserts, "to be in enjoyment or love at all times. Emotions and critical thoughts might temporarily trap you in a cycle of negativity and doubt, but you will be able to measure your growth by how quickly you return to clarity and self-love."[96]

Staying positive is always a choice. It's wise to remember that, as is frequently stated in LoA groups, "The Universe detests whiners."

3. Focus on the good in your life. Focusing only on the good and the positive in life will result in a gratifyingly different experience than continuing to respond like an amoeba with no conscious involvement. When your attention slips from the good, silently say "Cancel!" and bring your awareness back to what's good and positive.

Having a collection of "happy places," special memories, available whenever "something not so happy" comes along, can help make the switch easier and faster. Until your ability to switch focus from negative to positive becomes a habit, I recommend consciously creating such a list. Practice daily on little temptations to be thrown off-course, like the newspaper under your car, someone else using your dumpster for their dog poop, or a driver who pulls out in front of you or doesn't let you into the flow of traffic when your lane is about to run out. If you wait until you *really* need it, as when faced with an event that carries a high emotional charge, it would be too late.

If you subscribe to LoA, you choose whether to be happy or sad. It's a simple fact.

For example, if I'm feeling great and someone disappoints me, I can choose either to be right or to be happy. If I focus on their behavior and feel sorry for myself, I'm choosing to be a victim of someone else's behavior. Alternatively, I could simply accept that they get to choose their behavior just as I get to choose mine. In other words, I can allow them the life they choose, and choose to focus on the good stuff in mine. Pining over another person's choice will not change it, but the cost to your own life will be loss of happiness for however long you choose to dwell on their choice. If I ask you to dance and you choose not to accept, that's okay by me. There are other partners who will accept. The bottom line is simple: you get to choose what you want to think, what you want to believe, how you want to feel, and your choices affect your happiness.

You *can* choose to be either happy or sad. Why not choose to be happy?

4. Choose only positive thoughts. Remember "like attracts like," that what you choose to think about will attract more thoughts like it. If, for example, you choose to think about your lost love, the Universe will cheerfully send you millions more "like" thoughts so you can really get down. Understand that you're not the only one in the history of mankind who ever had that experience, that there are zillions more unhappy thoughts you can entertain if you choose to attract them. It's like that old saying, "Misery loves company."[97]

As you become aware of a thought, whether your own in response to something that just happened or one of the many that come in response to the thought on which you chose to focus, remember that choosing only positive ones is, in fact, the only real power we have. Faced with a negative thought, you have two choices: dwell on it, or switch your attention to something else like one of your happy memories or even that flower over there. When you first notice you're thinking becoming negative, withdraw your attention.

Again, we *can* choose to be happy or sad, think positively or negatively. It's within our power to feel happy most of the time. Why not try it? Be positive, expect only good things, and watch how your experience of life changes!

Andersen's "thirty-day mental diet," which stipulates "you are not to accept a single negative thought nor dwell on a single negative premise," is the clearest example of how to do that.[98] When you slip (as you will, of course), just start over as you would in changing any other addictive behavior. At this writing I'm on my tenth effort, but feeling more positive each day that soon I will be . . . even better at it!

5. Incorporate visualization into your life. While visualization is deemed critical to ordering up what you want from the Universe, it's also an important tool for living life on this planet. A handy way to practice is to perfectly rehearse an event in one's mind. For example, if you have a challenging business call to make, taking a moment to visualize what you'll say and how you'll say it can make a huge difference. If you're learning something new, like a Tai Chi sequence, mentally rehearsing it perfectly will help your mind remember it.

Visualization is especially useful in sports. When I broke my ankle and was off the tennis courts for an entire season, I practiced my game in my head. The next time I played on the courts, everyone remarked how much I had improved! Why had my game improved? Because I had only practiced doing it *right*. On the court, much of practice isn't. That was thirty years ago, and I still use visualization, a lot.

Recently, a friend told me about her experience in the Air Force and how she learned to parachute with visualization. The first step was imagining themselves doing the jump just as the instructor specified. The next step was acting as if they were jumping out of planes. Their practice was in tiny steps—in other words, the first "jump" was only in their minds; the first physical jump was only a few feet.

Seeing yourself happy, in love, successful in your work, and pursuing your heart's passion is the homework required to experience those things. Overcoming the resistance of disbelief and feelings of unworthiness is a tough challenge for most of us, but "acting as if" you are already experiencing your dream can help. In fact, your ability to become the thing you desire depends on this skill. Recall how Braden's Native American friend prayed for rain, how he imagined that it was, in fact, already raining.

6. Change your habitual responses. A particular response repeated in similar situations becomes habitual. Such responses literally carve ruts in our brains to make it easier to respond to the next situation like it. In their book, *Super Brain*, authors Rudolph Tanzi and Deepak Chopra explain how this ritualistic behavior affects us.

> Primitive reactions (fear, anger, jealousy, aggression) overrule the higher brain. Because our brains are imprinted with genetic memory over thousands of generations, the lower brain is still with us,

generating primitive and often negative drives like fear and anger. But the brain is constantly evolving, and we have gained the ability to master the lower brain through choice and free will.[99]

The human brain *has* evolved, and how it works has been studied by scientists. They have proven that we really can *choose* to be happy. Getting stuck in routine behaviors means that you'll always have the same response whenever a similar situation shows up. To step out of that limiting box, *Super Brain* authors offer these suggestions for "How To Be Adaptable."

Stop repeating what never worked in the first place.

Stand back and ask for a new solution.

Stop struggling at the level of the problem.

Work on your own stuckness [sic]. Don't worry about the other person.

When the old stressors are triggered, walk away.

See righteous anger for what it really is—destructive anger dressed up to sound positive.

Rebuild the bonds that have become frayed.

Take on more of the burden than you think you deserve.

Stop attaching so much weight to being right. In the grand scheme of things, being right is insignificant compared with being happy.[100]

7. Change your habits of mind. Timothy Gallwey presents a related, but different, perspective on the mind in his series of books about the "inner game" of different sports. He explains that inner game as what happens in the mind of the player, the game played against opponents, such as lapses in concentration, nervousness, self-doubt, and self-condemnation. Skills required to play this inner game include letting go of self-judgment, recognizing and trusting the natural learning process, and, above all, gaining practical experience in the art of concentration.

It doesn't take a wizard to see how this applies to LoA. Learning to "stay calm in the midst of rapid and unsettling changes"[101] is a skill absolutely required on the court (as cleverly depicted in the 2004 romantic comedy, *Wimbledon)*. Likewise, having a center of calm can help those using LoA to remain at ease and focused when the Universe responds to their pitched balls with a curve all its own. Observing what has happened instead of freaking out enables one to deal with challenges as merely extra steps that weren't anticipated. The response then becomes: "Oh. Okay. I can do that."

8. Choose a proven plan for success. If I had a particular goal, I'd choose one of the proven plans for success because I've had personal experience with some and know they work. For example, I got through a complicated doctoral research program in the 70s with the Program Evaluation and Review Technique (P.E.R.T.), which involves (1) breaking big projects down into small steps based on experience (yours or someone else's), (2) identifying resources (people, things, places), and (3) displaying all of this in symbols (I used circles) on a timeline (each ensuing step dependent upon completion of the preceding one), which you get to color as each task is completed.

One of my former junior high students, then a freshman at the university, helped me make a flow chart on a piece of butcher paper that wrapped around the walls of my office. This placed the project in clear view so I always knew where I stood with it, as did anyone else coming into my office! Talk about accountability!

P.E.R.T., routine for anyone in business, at least in the 70s, originated in the military. It was used to get the Polaris submarine under the ice to the extreme end of the earth and back, prepped for unexpected events, and without running out of anything including toilet paper and fresh air. It's a planning technique that can get you where you want to go if you can identify the requisite steps and resources.

How is P.E.R.T. related to using the Law of Attraction? It's a way to keep you on track towards your goal and it will also will help you do your part, not only by identifying steps and resources, but also by breaking those steps into doable tasks with deadlines to keep you focused. A focused mind is less likely to spiral down into "I don't deserve this, there's no way this is going to work, blah, blah, blah." When your mind starts to dive, just look at your next step and get busy.

If what you want is something specific like a new career or more money, consider trying one of the programs mentioned in Chapter 2—like Hill's *Laws of Success in Sixteen Lessons*, Cole-Whittaker's "Seven Steps to the Spiritual and Material Riches of Life" in *Think and Grow Rich*, Dooley's *Leveraging the Universe and Engaging the Magic,* or Gaines' *Four Laws of Spiritual Prosperity*—not only because they are proven plans, but because each of these authors provides ample personal experience stories to guide the reader.

If you want something less "material"—like rain or world peace—then of all those approaches for conscious co-creating, prayer is still the best technique. Consider experimenting with different forms of prayer. Chapter 2 identifies a couple, (1) Bible: ask, say thanks, have faith, and believe it has already been given, and (2) Braden's "5th mode of prayer": acknowledge what you have chosen, feel that it is already accomplished, and give thanks for the opportunity to choose.[102] (They're pretty much the same, but sometimes a different word or phrase makes a huge difference in one's understanding.)

Since I started this project, I have tracked my prayers. The concept of "already done" had been missing from mine before. Now, when I include that concept in my prayers—already been given, already done—I emerge highly motivated and energized. I can't wait to start doing my part! Now I realize that it is the evidence of faith Jesus tried to teach! It also happens to be the key element in the "treatments" dispensed by professional metaphysicians.

9. Keep it to yourself. Don't talk about your goals with anyone unless you are involved with a small Mastermind Group in which every member is doing what you're doing. No one else will understand, and you don't need advice or negative thinking about what you're doing.

If you must share, but don't have such a group, create a special journal to establish your goals, track your progress, and pour your heart out when you get stuck.

10. Team up with your Silent Partner. Once you've identified the steps to get wherever you want to go, either from experience or by asking someone who has done it before, try listing your part in one column of a folded sheet of paper and listing in the other column those things that are beyond your control, that must be taken on faith. Focus on your side until you're done, then check and see how much of the Silent Partner's side remains.

I used that technique when I was leaving Shawnigan Lake, B.C. in 1990, the end of my walkabout, to return home to Colorado. The friend with whom I'd been staying had wanted me to stay, as did I, but there were so many . . . details that would have to be resolved. So I asked her to join me at her picnic table outside and watch as I listed all the things that would have to happen for my return to be possible. Some were "miracles," like sell my house in a seriously depressed market. No one was selling because no one was buying. I wanted her to understand that I would do my best and the outcome depended on things I could not control.

Before leaving on the three-day journey back home I phoned and asked my Realtor to list the house. Within three weeks, in a depressed real estate market, my house sold and I had gotten rid of almost everything inside in a one-day moving sale with "unexpected" help from people I didn't know had been friends! I returned to B.C. with the money from the moving sale.

Before you sleep, have a chat with your subconscious mind. Include gratitude for all the good you've experienced over your lifetime and ask for what you want now. As an Alchemical Hypnotherapist, I learned to "talk to myself," to my inner guides and sub-personalities (archetypes), to get everyone on board for a change I wanted to make.

Recall that Mangan suggests a similar approach in his book about the Subconscious and the switchwords he discovered that activate it. He emphasizes the importance of submission to self-union, to the bigger you, and the switchword for that is "Together." Try chanting that word to yourself, silently, twenty-eight times as fast as you can. Note how you feel afterwards, and what you feel inclined to do.

11. "Act as if." If there's a change you want to make in your life, follow Cole-Whittaker's advice and find, and model, someone who exemplifies that change. Dress like they dress, speak like they speak. I realized, for example, that as a former workaholic my casual social skills were underdeveloped. To amend that, I have taken to observing others who seem to have mastered conversational small talk. Although I never see myself engaging much in this with anyone, I do, finally, see the value in beginning a conversation with, "Hi, how are you?"

If you're feeling blue, lift the corners of your mouth. Stand up straight and pull your shoulders back. Notice how you feel.

If you don't have the energy to do the thing that needs to be done, imagine it already done; notice how you feel now about doing it and get started. If you feel that no one likes you, quit thinking about yourself and go help someone you don't even know. Act as if you already are what you want to be and you'll notice important changes. Try it, and record your experience.

12. Heal yourself with Inner Child work. Some of the respondents to my little study remarked that people fail in their use of LoA because they don't feel worthy, because they have low self-esteem. One way to deal with this is by claiming your Inner Child. Several options are available. You could do it yourself with, for example, John Bradshaw's work, which includes recordings, videos, and books on healing the Inner Child. For those who prefer a one-on-one approach, a psychotherapist certified in Alchemical Hypnotherapy might be the answer. Inner Child work involves accepting responsibility for that child (for yourself). It involves promising to love, protect, listen to, and spend time each day with the Inner Child, not because it's cute, but because it's the key to all other archetypes or personalities in the subconscious mind that affect our behavior. This is the one who can make or break your efforts for success. Ever heard of sabotage?

My journey to loving myself began in the 70's when I was in graduate school. I had discovered Fritz Perls' *Gestalt Therapy* and had been doing my personal version of his work–alone, in my living room, with the drapes closed. I'd set up two chairs facing one another. Sitting in one, I'd be my adult self, talking to the little girl inside, my self as a child, who I imagined sitting in the other chair. After expressing myself as an adult, I'd switch chairs and respond through the voice of that little girl to the adult who had just spoken. That process would continue, back and forth, back and forth, until whatever was "up" had been resolved.

When I began training to be an Alchemical Hypnotherapist, in 1991, having already had many years of practice in "make believe" communications, I found it easy to join in the conversation of all those sub-personalities talking inside my head. I was also, at that time, reading and listening to John Bradshaw's work on the Inner Child.

Doing Inner Child work, learning to love yourself, begins with accepting that you do, in fact, have an Inner Child, and realizing that that little person could easily be very angry with you. Mine definitely was.

Forming a relationship with that younger part of yourself involves listening to what your inner self wants and needs from you, then being the stand-up adult and delivering instead of wantonly projecting that need onto others you hope will fix your relationship. (Mine wanted me to get out of a very destructive relationship, one that didn't even feel safe, much less loving.)

No one had a perfect childhood, but as an adult, each of us can become the perfect parent to our self, our own Inner Child. This relationship is the foundation for all other relationships, the means for bringing a whole person to the party. Two whole people, each on solid ground, have a completely different relationship from the sinking sand of two wounded people.

13. Clear old beliefs with Tapping. Tapping specific meridian points while saying phrases relevant to whatever needs healing briefly describes the Emotional Freedom Technique you can learn online. This group has plenty of Web sites and You Tube videos to help you master the skill. Of particular relevance to those using LoA to attract abundance is a book by Carol Look, *Attracting Abundance with EFT*.

14. Forgive yourself. The best place to begin forgiveness is with your self. We seem to have such a need to punish ourselves. We make a mistake and let it haunt us, sometimes our entire lives! There is another way. We can simply accept that we did what we did acting on what we knew at the time. Whenever negative thoughts about mistakes you made in the past surface, try this simple mantra: "I did the best I could with the information, knowledge, and guidance I had at the time."

Consider also using decrees from St. Germain to purify yourself, to get rid of negativity, as written by Mark and Elizabeth Clare Prophet in *The Science of the Spoken Word*. Try beginning with "I AM a being of violet fire! I AM the purity God desires!"[103] Repetitions of decrees are recommended first thing in the morning and last thing at night, just as affirmations are, but I also do mine when walking.

15. Forgive others. Extend your forgiveness to anyone you imagine has hurt you. No sane person starts out each morning with the goal of hurting people, but it happens. Sadly, when one responds with anger or a grudge, the only one being hurt is himself. On the relationship between thoughts, feelings, and the impact they have on the body, New Thought leader Louise Hay wrote, in *You Can Heal Your Life*, about her experience with cancer and how she healed herself with forgiveness.

Perhaps her best-known book is "the little blue book" published in 1976, which provides an easy reference for mental causes for physical conditions. Noteworthy is her identification of criticism, anger, resentment, and guilt as the mental thought patterns that cause most diseases. The organization of this little book is very user-friendly: three columns, including "Problem," "Probable Cause" (mental equivalent), and "New Thought Pattern" (healing affirmation).

Use E.P.C. and visualization to forgive. My journey with forgiveness began in 1988 when I spent a full year trying to forgive this person of authority in my workplace who seemed committed to driving me off campus. I had read dozens of books about forgiveness, listened to as many recordings, but still could make no headway in forgiving her. Finally, I tried a technique I'd learned from Sanaya Roman, one that utilizes both visualization and what I learned as E.P.C., communicating with others . . . in your mind.

> Think of someone you'd like to communicate with. Get quiet, and imagine a fine gridwork of light around you, extending straight upward. Next, imagine a line of light going out from your heart to this person's. Mentally tell this person that you love and accept him or her exactly as he or she is. Express any other messages of love you want to send.[104]

Forgiveness and letting go of the hurtful experience might be the biggest obstacles to success with LoA. How can you be in the positive flow connected with Source when you're harboring enmity? However long it takes, it's definitely worth it to master this one. True confession: It's the hardest lesson I ever learned; it took years.

16. Reclaim all the power you gave away. This sounds difficult, but it's not. You can do it in a visualization experience by imagining the mistakes you think you made and/or the people you believe "hurt you." It's also good even when it's just time to move on in some way.

Of the many versions available, what works for me is the one I learned in '89 from one of my favorite Tarot books, *MOTHERPEACE*. While the quoted passage is specific to the "death" of a relationship, you can modify it for other endings, like leaving a job. Here's the process of "psychic cleansing you can use to affirm and speed the process of letting go."

Take some quiet time and remember the relationship fully, allowing your tears and pain to release. You may want to look at old pictures, listen to old music you shared, gather together objects given to you by your former lover. Let the feelings flow freely and completely. At some point you will have a sense of completion (or exhaustion).

Then breathe deeply and find a quiet place of meditation inside your mind. Visualize or think about the cords or ties that have connected you to this other person. They appear like electric cords or cords to a switchboard, from your body to the other person's form. You can look at each separate cord and decide what it represents, then pull it or cut it. Or you can simply take a look at the whole thing, and cut all the cords at once. As you pull or cut the cords, make a strong affirmation, such as, "I am letting go of so-and-so with love. I acknowledge the Death of this relationship. It is completed."

Then sit and meditate on the Motherpeace Death card for a while, letting the image of the snake shedding its skin sink into your psyche. Feel your fears about Death sliding away with the old skin and allow your new self to emerge like the gentle changing of the seasons.[105]

Author Vicki Noble says that if we use this process when any form of death enters our lives, we'll be like the shaman who has mastered death and no longer fears it Again, "death" refers to that which has ended, whether it is a job, a relationship, or an actual transition to death.

17. Quit judging others. Understand that whatever you see in another is merely an out-picturing or projection of what's inside yourself. We are all mirrors for each other. If you say to your friend, "You're so negative!", realize that you are, in fact, expressing out loud what is true about yourself. Really understanding this one thing will change your life.

Earlier, in the section on Hick's contributions to LoA, you read about the need to see joy everywhere and why it's in our best interest to allow everyone to be however they choose (Please see Chapter 5, or, better yet, read her books!).

Similarly, in *Walking between the Worlds: The Science of Compassion*, Braden writes about recognizing our deepest fears, learning from the reflections of our innermost and outer selves that we see in others (the seven mirrors from the Essenes), and what it means to have compassion. He explains what those "charges" (a.k.a. "buttons" or "triggers") really mean and how you can transform them using the Seven Essene Mirrors of Relationship.

1. Reflections of the Moment
2. Reflections of Judgment
3. Reflections of Loss
4. Reflections of Your Most Forgotten Love,
5. Reflections of Father/Mother/Creator
6. Reflections of Your Quest into Darkness
7. Your Greatest Act of Compassion.

For example, recall that one motivation for doing my thesis on LoA was to sing the Na-Na song to those self-appointed LoA cops who assail their friends with how negative they are. A quick self-exam ("Do I do that?") reminded me that I had done something similar in my own exuberance over something recently learned, as when I told my walking partner that she was leading with her head and could expect neck, shoulder, and hip issues if she didn't change that pattern now. I was so proud of what I'd learned in movement therapy I wanted to share it with everyone all the time. She never complained, but having been on the receiving end of that behavior I can see how she might have felt I was out of line. *Guilty! I have done that very same thing! Issue resolved.*

Using the Seven Mirrors is one of the best ways to resolve relationship challenges. Clarity for "dark nights of the soul" resulting from such challenges can empower you to feel safe and equipped to deal with whatever shows up. You might even get clear on your relationship with your creator. For more about this topic, consider viewing Braden's videos, especially *Walking Between the Worlds*, and reading his book, *Walking Between The Worlds: The Science of Compassion.*

18. Change your mind. Remember when a friend called to ask if you wanted to do something like go for a hike and you said "No" because you just didn't feel like it? Remember how your friend left the invitation open and gave you an opportunity to reconsider by replying, "OK, but if you change your mind . . ." Remember how, after that call, you began thinking about what it would feel like to be outdoors, breathing crisp air, feeling your muscles adjust your balance to the uneven rocks under your shoes, the silence like a healing bath to your frayed nerves, the thrill of spotting that critter way high in the tree having a nap in the forked limbs, and it all felt so good that you called back immediately to say, "If it's not to late, I'm in!"

That's a simple example of changing your mind. You do it every day. It's exactly the same process as staying positive whatever the challenge you're facing now. Think about it.

19. Clean up the mess! When we're surrounded by clutter and disarray, our thoughts and feelings begin to reflect that state. Get rid of what you don't use, what no longer serves you. Don't worry about how much you'll get for it or whether you're giving it to the right person. Just get it out of your space. Create an order that works for you, not against you. Spend an afternoon simply cleaning. For example, take everything out of your closet, pretend you're at a store and choose what you want, then put the rest in a box and get it out of your living space. Clean that area with such love that you couldn't imagine doing it any other way. When you finish, notice how you feel, not only today, but also each time you open that closet door. Order and cleanliness are requisite to clear thinking and staying positive. How can you feel positive when you can't find that thing you need right this second because your digs are so disturbingly disheveled?

20. Listen to your body. You get one earth-suit for this great adventure called life. It's built to last, ever re-generating, but only if you take care of it. One set of rules for taking care of the body can be found in *Book One of The Essene Gospel of Peace*, translated by Edmond Bordeaux Szekely.

The body is so much more than a portable platform for your head. For example, it has wisdom beyond what your brain can understand or offer. Author Hicks alludes to body wisdom when she advises readers to use their "Emotional Guidance System," to focus on "good feelings." Others counsel us to pay attention to how "it" feels. For example, before making important decisions, imagine each option and attend to how your body responds. If you experience tightening or tension or a just plain icky feeling, that option probably isn't in your best interest at this time.

Massage therapists, acupuncturists, Chinese medicine doctors, and yoga teachers tell us that the body remembers everything, that our memories are stored in our bodies. Part of the treatment from such a therapist might include the directions to recall the situation in sensory detail, to really feel it, to talk about what it meant for you, then breathe and see how it feels. Maybe you'll notice how it's changed, or that it's even completely gone!

Storing memories and their associated feelings in our bodies can engender such circumstances as crippling body pain and disease. Our success or failure using the law of attraction to co-create our heart's desire depends on our ability to stay positive, which is difficult to do in the presence of raging bodily pain . We must be able to quickly drop what feels bad in order to be able to choose something positive to think about instead.

More important, regarding LoA, is that such vivid visualization required for that healing is the same ability to *become that which we desire*, to imagine it so completely that we also experience the associated feelings and the resultant joy of this gift we give thanks for as we accept as already done.

Pop quiz: If the law of attraction means that whatever you think about with feeling is attracted to you, then what do you suppose happens when you notice something you don't like and keep thinking about it with feeling? What do you think happens when you allow yourself to not only be irritated by something when it is happening, but long afterwards? Just saying.

Body focus is also essential to the Release Technique (a.k.a. Sedona method) developed by Lester Levenson, which calls for continued releasing of any kind of resistance we might have so that our energy flows freely. Recall, for example, a situation that didn't feel good and notice where in the body you feel it (generally, either the chest or stomach), then allow that feeling to release through an imaginary tube to the outside. What Levenson discovered is that when our energy flows without resistance we become "Superconductors," able to accomplish great things effortlessly and with ease.

Try this now by imagining a goal you want to achieve and noticing any feelings of resistance in your body. You might notice fear, doubt, and frustration, even anger. Any feeling that is not positive and empowering is a form of resistance. This little exercise certainly does not equate to "knowing" the Release Technique. My intention, again, is simply to share what's out there, what's worked for me. His student, Larry Crane, offers Levenson's work online through recordings, workshops, and groups.

Using the law of attraction to consciously co-create with LoA formulas is much too complex for most people to experience success out of the gate. It depends on far too much including (1) accepting full responsibility for one's life, (2) understanding how thoughts work and using the power of thought consciously, (3) understanding and using the power of visualization, (4) accepting that most of the time, unless we are enlightened masters, we must do our part in the creation of material things as specified by most LoA formulas, (5) letting the manifestation happen in its perfect time and maintaining a steadfast belief, in the face of sensory feedback that might suggest otherwise, that it is already here now, and (6) according to my research, becoming aligned with Good, following whatever rules are ordained by your particular spiritual path. If you don't have a spiritual practice, consider using the Golden Rule and treat everyone, including how you think about or talk about them, the way you'd like to be treated.

If success in using LoA relied only on successfully manipulating formulas, simple practice with doing it differently, with finding the method that works for you, would be enough. Obviously, it isn't.

My intention with sharing these particular twenty techniques is to underline that our success in LoA is not contingent only upon our understanding and use of the formulas. It also depends on how we think, feel and believe about ourselves and all others. Doing the personal work can help clear the way to having your life more like you want it, more of the time.

Chapter 10

Impact of the Study
On You, Me, Maybe the World

A welcome result of this little survey was the realization of the impact it had had on those who had chosen to participate in it. I first noticed this as I was collecting surveys at the Fellowship of Spirit. The revelations on both sides felt as if we had been stumbling around in the dark, and someone had just turned on the light. Many of the participants touched my arm and shared personal insights as they handed me their survey.

"I don't have to be a victim."

"I can change my experience merely by changing my thoughts."

"I not only *can* actively participate in the creation of my own life, but *am invited to do that in the Bible!*"

Suddenly, I realized that, standing starkly alone, those comments revealed profound concepts. Not only that, but I knew that if the speakers assimilated what they had learned about themselves, and practiced what they had learned about how life on this planet works, the effect on their lives would be immediately felt.

The implications for society are even greater. Just imagine a society where everyone accepted responsibility for his or her actions! Imagine being in a community where each member understood the consequences of his thoughts! Consider how empowering it would be if young people learned the relationship of their thoughts to what they experience—while they're still young!

Finally, I was able to re-think my position about those doing LoA groups and classes as "just another hot idea to get more stuff." Like others who have scoffed at the popularity of the Law of Attraction, saying that only greedy people would be interested in LoA, and that it's an obstacle to spiritual growth (as I had done), I now realized that there's another way to see it: as a simple formula that includes rules for living the best possible life on plant earth. A sort of cheat-sheet from the wisdom of the Bible and other ancient teachings.

Not only that, but ultimately, I saw LoA as a tiny indicator of the evolution of humanity. As more and more people learn about it, the impact on the entire human race and all of our lives could be affected in a very positive way.

Now I saw that by engaging in such activities, each participant would have the opportunity to grow spiritually in a way that perhaps was not heretofore offered on their path.

Just as those wonderful people at that tiny church had revealed such huge revelations simply by taking a five-minute survey, I now could see community groups sharing their experience of practicing positive thinking, and learning and growing from one another. And my judgment about their motivation—it's only greed, wanting to get more stuff—I now saw as invalid, too. Haven't I professed that I wanted more knowledge and insight about LoA? "Wanting more" is in our genes. It's what we do. It's why we're here: to create. We just express it differently.

And, for those bothered by the "fact" that it works equally for all, I have to ask, "Why are you concerned with what someone else is doing?" There is no need to be concerned about those who are only interested in "getting more stuff," because that's their life and the natural consequences of having all that stuff are also theirs. Keep your eye on your own garden.

But that's not the only jolt of larger meaning I received from doing this little study. As I was immersed in re-reading sources to find responses to participants' comments, the relationship of all my previous experiences—like Christianity, Tarot, Builders of the Adytum Mystery School, and yoga—came into sharp focus.

Suddenly I saw those diverse experiences as having one thing in common—they each had contributed to my unquestioned belief in a Superior Power that had guided me all my days. In an instant, I finally understood how all the tangents of my spiritual life were related. I realized it was all leading me to this moment—even the Vision Quests with Huichol Indians in the Mexican Desert where I saw the energy grid that ties everything together, saw that, in fact, everything is all One thing!

As for my study, while all the older sources I used included something about that aspect, becoming One with Source, only the ancient texts and New Thought books made it their total argument. While Hicks included "The Art of Allowing" as part of her formula and continually states that one must be aligned "with that which he desires," that's not quite the same as *you must realize that the power for creation is not yours, but is due to the Power that created All things,* and that *you must align yourself with God,* or even, as Neville puts it, you must claim that you are, indeed One with God: "I AM GOD."

Just to show you how fast IT works, this very morning, when I declared "I am so done with this project because I have so much other stuff to do that has been neglected," I also got my daily email from the Hicks website, including this statement, *"A state of appreciation is pure Connection to Source where there is no perception of lack.* (Excerpted from the workshop: Money and the Law of Attraction on August 31, 2008). (In my world, that's called a "Cosmic Thump.")

And this, I believe, is the most important reason why people fail, if not *the* missing link—the part of the manifesting process people have somehow failed to grasp. Coming into alignment begins with facing our confusion about God. What is it we really believe? Is God "a man in a white suit up there?" Is God "merely energy" as one participant commented? Or is God something else entirely?

On this sticky issue, I have nothing to offer, because I believe it's a personal and very private deal for most people. And, I'm not willing to entertain debates about how anyone chooses to understand such an intense question. It's part of each person's journey to figure it out for himself. Everyone gets to choose what he or she wishes to believe. If you believe "it's all just energy" as one online participant stated, that's cool. If you're okay with the stock market, your intellectuality, or your own hard labor as your god, and that works for you, that's also cool, and that's not the point.

The point is this: as long as one believes God *is that man up there*, he tends to refuse responsibility for his experience, because it's too easy to say, "It wasn't God's will," or "I'm being punished by God," or some other Old Testament excuse. And that is not consistent with the basic requirement of LoA, to accept responsibility for everything you experience.

If, on the other hand, we begin to embrace the concept that God (however you understand that concept) is ALL THAT IS, and therefore must be also within us, then we can begin to move towards embracing the full ramifications of that perspective.

How you choose to name your god is irrelevant. If you choose to acknowledge that there is Something Bigger than you, it doesn't matter whether you label your god Energy or Spirit or Shiva or The Subconscious Mind or God. If you agree that your god is omnipresent (everywhere) it is logical to realize that you must also be part of all THAT. And, of course, if you accept that you *are* a part of ALL THAT, then you must also accept that everyone else is, too, including that group you have issues with, including those guys on the other side of the planet, including, well, everyone and everything. And then you totally get why the Golden Rule is such a profound concept and why the gist of it appears in all religions.

Accepting that there is a power bigger than ourselves of whom/which we are a part enables us to take the next step and to realize that as such, we live and move and have our being in THAT. We might even come to believe, as God is within, that we also are intended to be creators: "As above, so below." But *only* when we acknowledge and embrace the God/Universe within, because it is THAT which does the actual creating.

As Andersen asserted, we create nothing; God does. Instead, as mortals, "These are the tools we deal with: we think; we love; and we believe. Through thought we attain knowledge. Through love we attune ourselves with Universal Mind. Through belief we transform thoughts into things. These three tools, understood and used, bring power."[106]

It seems obvious that until and unless one faces their own concept of God/All-That-Is/Energy, and gets clear on how they relate to her, this will be a troublesome area that creates fuss in trying to use the LoA. For non-believers, as a start, consider the possibility that the stuff that is the basis of All That Is, actually, is All That Is *Good*. That little shift is actually huge. Think about it.

Either way, the popularity of formulas for consciously creating with the spiritual law of attraction is not a fad that will go away. And I'm okay with that. I no longer despise it. As for those who attack their friends with "The Law," I simply choose to see them as little children, excited about their new, shiny toy. Just as I have been and probably will be again. They'll get there soon enough. We all will. We're all just bozos on the same bus (a nod to Ram Das).

I now see the advent of LoA as another intrusion to the consciousness of man, another invitation to wake up. It could even, possibly, mark a tiny evolutionary step of man learning to stand upright instead of swinging from trees. As mankind learns more about LoA, studies its origins, keeps working with it, and actually living those principles, not only does the individual's life improve, but, by the impact of their sheer numbers, they also help to raise the consciousness of all mankind!

Imagine a world where everyone understood that their thoughts attracted similar thoughts—not only from others, but also from all thoughts that had ever happened. Picture world governance wherein politicians realized that they think, say, and do nothing in secret—that the veil has dropped, and all their actions, even the ones in their heads, are as transparent as clear glass. Consider what it would be like if everyone were connected to All That Is Good and lived their lives based on the principle of the Golden Rule. In other words, what if everyone embraced these elements of The LoA formula as a way of life?

Thank you for going the distance on this little journey with me. If you took away one useful thing, I reckon it's been worth it. It was for me. The trick is in the application. Let's both pick one thing we learned to create a better life, and let's do it today!

Notes

¹ B.O.T.A. Builders of the Adytum. http://www.bota.org September 9, 2014.

² B.O.T.A., *Highlights of Tarot* (Los Angeles, CA: Builders of the Adytum, 1970) 8.

³ Paul Case, *The Tarot* (Richmond, VA: Macoy Publishing Company, 1947) 15.

⁴ Case 7.

⁵ Dr. Ann Davies, *This Is the Truth about the Self* (Los Angeles, CA: Builders of the Adytum, Ltd., 1960) 4.

⁶ Davies 12.

⁷ Mitch Horowitz, *One Simple Idea* (New York: Crown Publishers, 2014). Kindle file.

⁸ U.S. Andersen, *Three Magic Words* (Hollywood, CA: Wilshire Book Company, 1954).

⁹ John-Roger and Peter McWilliams, *Life 101* (Los Angeles, CA: Prelude Press, 1990) 39.

¹⁰ Greg Braden, *The Isaiah Effect* (New York: Three Rivers Press, 2000) 148.

¹¹ *The Holy Bible, English Standard Version* (Crossway Bibles, 2011) Kindle file.

¹² *The Holy Bible, ESV*

¹³ Doron Alon, *The Bible and The Law of Attraction* (USA: Numinosity Press, 2009).

¹⁴ Alon.

¹⁵ Alon.

[16] Alon.

[17] Steven L. Hairfield, *A Metaphysical Interpretation of the Bible* (Spirit Works Publishing, 2013) 798.

[18] Eric Butterworth, *Spiritual Economics* (Unity Village, MO: Unity School of Christianity, 1989) 25.

[19] Andersen 193.

[20] Napoleon Hill, *The Law of Success* (Meriden, CT: The Ralston University Press, 1928). Kindle file.

[21] Hill.

[22] Hill.

[23] Hill, *The Law of Success in Sixteen Lessons*, Lessons 14-16 (Cleveland, OH: The Ralston Society, 1947) 149.

[24] William Walker Atkinson, *Thought Vibration* (Memphis, TN: General Books LLC, 2012) 4.

[25] Goddard, *Your Faith Is Your Fortune* (Camarillo, CA: DeVorss Publications, 1941) 159.

[26] Goddard 32.

[27] Goddard 33.

[28] U.S. Andersen, *Three Magic Words* (Hollywood, CA: Wilshire Book Company, 1954) 193.

[29] Andersen 194.

[30] Andersen 199.

[31] Andersen 201.

[32] Andersen 63.

[33] Andersen 143.

[34] Andersen 242.

[35] James T. Mangan, *The Secret of Perfect Living* (Englewood Cliffs, NJ: Prentice-Hall, 1963) 3.

[36] Mangan 174.

[37] Mangan 221-222.

[38] Mangan 223.

[39] Esther and Jerry Hicks, *The Law of Attraction* (Carlsbad, CA: Hay House, Inc., 2006) 24.

[40] Hicks 120.

[41] Hicks 120.

[42] Esther and Jerry Hicks, *Ask and It Is Given* (Carlsbad, CA: Hay House, Inc., 2004) 47.

[43] Hicks 48.

[44] Hicks 127.

[45] Goddard 25

[46] Terry Cole-Whittaker, *Every Saint Has a Past, Every Sinner, a Future* (New York: Jeremy P. Tarcher, 2001) 153.

[47] Cole-Whittaker 153.

[48] Cole-Whittaker 78.

[49] Cole-Whittaker 151.

[50] Cole-Whittaker 150.

[51] Cole-Whittaker 115.

[52] Cole-Whittaker 119.

[53] Cole-Whittaker 241.

[54] Cole-Whittaker 274.

[55] Mike Dooley, *Leveraging the Universe and Engaging the Magic* (Simon and Schuster Audio Division, 2008).

[56] Butterworth 180.

[57] Butterworth 181.

[58] Butterworth 176.

[59] Edwene Gaines, *The Four Spiritual Laws of Prosperity* (New York: Rodale, 2005) 1-2.

[60] Hill, *The Law of Success*, 180

[61] Hill, *Think and Grow Rich*, 36.

[62] Andersen 167.

[63] Mangan 152.

[64] Andersen 65.

[65] Roosevelt, Brainy Quotes, http://www.brainyquote.com/quotes/quotes/t/theodorero100965.html.

[66] Hicks 99.

[67] Atkinson 5.

[68] Andersen 210.

[69] Cole-Whittaker 150.

[70] Cole-Whittaker 150.

[71] Cole-Whittaker 150.

[72] Alon 63.

[73] Alon 67.

[74] Goddard 33.

[75] Andersen 20.

[76] Andersen 23.

[77] Braden 188-189.

[78] Braden 149.

[79] Braden 150.

[80] Braden 154.

[81] Braden 166-167.

[82] *The Living Bible*, Matthew 21:21-22.

[83] Cole-Whittaker 89.

[84] Alon location 137.

[85] Braden 167.

[86] Alon location 68.

[87] Cole-Whittaker 150.

[88] Braden 218.

[89] Braden 199.

[90] Goddard 33.

[91] Andersen 194.

[92] Andersen 195.

[93] Mangan 52-53.

[94] Peggy Dylan Burkan, *Guiding Yourself to a Spiritual Reality* (Twin Harte, CA: Reunion Press, 1984) 1.

[95] Burkan 4.

[96] Burkan 4.

[97] "misery loves company." *The American Heritage® Dictionary of Idioms by Christine Ammer*. Houghton Mifflin Company. 08 Oct. 2014. <Dictionary.com http://dictionary.reference.com/browse/misery loves company>.

[98] Andersen 172.

[99] Deepak Chopra, M.D. and Rudolph E. Tanzi, Ph.D., *Super Brain* (New York: Harmony Books, 2012) 19.

[100] Chopra and Tanzi 49.

[101] W. Timothy Gallwey, *The Inner Game of Tennis* (New York: Random House, 1974) 131.

[102] Braden 167.

[103] Mark L. and Elizabeth Clare Prophet, *The Science of the Spoken Word* (Summit University Press, 1965) ii.

[104] Sanaya Roman, *Spiritual Growth: Being Your Higher Self* (Tiburon, CA: HJ Kramer, Inc., 1989) 65.

[105] Vicki Noble, *Motherpeace* (San Francisco: Harper & Row, 1983) 104-105.

[106] Andersen 242.

Works Cited

Alon, Doron, *The Bible and The Law of Attraction*. USA: Numinosity Press, 2009. Kindle file.

Andersen, U.S. *Three Magic Words*. Hollywood, CA: Wilshire Book Company, 1954.

Atkinson, William Walker. *Thought Vibration or the Law of Attraction in the Thought World.* (Originally published in 1902 by New Thought Journal). Memphis, TN: General Books LLC, 2012.

The Holy Bible. English Standard Version (ESV). Crossway Bibles, A division of Good News Publishers, 2001.

B.O.T.A. Builders of the Adytum. http://www.bota.org September 9, 2014.

B.O.T.A., *Highlights of Tarot*. Los Angeles, CA: Builders of the Adytum, 1970.

Braden, Gregg. *The Isaiah Effect: Decoding the Lost Science of Prayer and Prophecy*. New York: Three Rivers Press, 2000.

Braden, Gregg. *Walking between the Worlds: The Science of Compassion*. Bellevue, WA: Radio Bookstore Press, 1997.

Burkan, Peggy Dylan. *Guiding Yourself Into A Spiritual Reality: Workbook*. Twain Harte, CA: Reunion Press, 1984.

Butterworth, Eric. *Spiritual Economics: the Prosperity Process*. Unity Village, MO: Unity School of Christianity, 1989.

Case, Paul. *The Tarot*. Richmond, VA: Macoy Publishing Company, 1947.

Cole-Whittaker, Terry. *Every Saint Has A Past, Every Sinner, A Future: Seven Steps to the Spiritual and Material Riches of Life*. New York: Jeremy P. Tarcher, 2001.

Davies, Dr. Ann. *This Is The Truth About The Self.* Los Angeles, CA: Builders of The Adytum, LTD., 1960.

Dooley, Mike. *Infinite Possibilities*: *The Art of Living Your Dreams*. New York: Simon and Schuster, 2009. Audio book.

Dooley, Mike. *Leveraging the Universe and Engaging the Magic*. Simon and Schuster Audio Division, 2008. Audio book.

Dooley, Mike: *Leveraging the Universe: 7 Steps to Engaging Life's Magic*. Atria Books/Beyond Words Publishing, Inc., 2011.

Gaines, Edwene. *The Four Spiritual Laws of Prosperity: A Simple Guide to Unlimited Abundance.* New York: Rodale, 2005.

Gallwey, W. Timothy. *The Inner Game of Tennis.* NY: Random House, 1974.

Hairfield, Ph.D., Steven L. *A Metaphysical Interpretation of the Bible.* Spirit Works Publishing, 2013.

Hicks, Esther and Jerry. *Ask and It Is Given: Learning to Manifest Your Desires.* Carlsbad, CA: Hay House, 2004.

Hicks, Esther and Jerry. *The Law of Attraction: The Basics of the Teachings of Abraham.* Carlsbad, CA: Hay House, 2006.

Hill, Napoleon. *The Law of Success in Sixteen Lessons.* Meriden, CONN: The Ralston University Press, 1928. Kindle file

Hill, Napoleon. *The Law of Success In Sixteen Lessons, Lessons 14-16* Cleveland, OH: The Ralston Society, 1947.

Hill, Napoleon. *Think and Grow Rich.* New York: Ballantine Books, 1937.

Horowitz, Mitch. *One Simple Idea.* New York: Crown Publishers, 2014. Kindle file

Lazaris: The Secrets of Manifesting What You Want.
Fairfax, CA: Concept-Synergy, 1985. Videocassette

Mangan, James T. *The Secret of Perfect Living.* Englewood
Cliffs, N.J.: Prentice-Hall, Inc., 1963.

McWilliams, John-Roger and Peter. *Life 101: Everything
We Wish We Had Learned In School—But Didn't.*
Los Angeles, CA.: Prelude Press, 1990.

"misery loves company." *The American Heritage®
Dictionary of Idioms by Christine Ammer.*
Houghton Mifflin Company. 08 Oct. 2014.
<Dictionary.com
http://dictionary.reference.com/browse/misery loves
company>.

Neville. *Your Faith Is Your Fortune.* Camarillo, CA:
DeVorss Publications, 1941.

Noble, Vicki. *Motherpeace: A Way to the Goddess through
Myth, Art, and Tarot* (San Francisco, CA: Harper &
Row, 1983), 104-105.

Prophet, Mark L. and Elizabeth Clare. *The Science of The
Spoken Word.*(Summit University press, 1965).

Roman, Sanaya. *Spiritual Growth: Being Your Higher Self*
(Tiburon, CA: HJ Kramer Inc., 1989), 65.

Made in the USA
Charleston, SC
09 January 2015